Mallarmé and the Art of Being Difficult

MALCOLM BOWIE

CAMBRIDGE UNIVERSITY PRESS

CAMBRIDGE

LONDON · NEW YORK · MELBOURNE

Published by the Syndics of the Cambridge University Press
The Pitt Building, Trumpington Street, Cambridge CB2 1RP
Bentley House, 200 Euston Road, London NW1 2DB
32 East 57th Street, New York, NY 10022, USA
296 Beaconsfield Parade, Middle Park, Melbourne 3206, Australia

First published 1978

Printed in Great Britain
by W & J Mackay Limited, Chatham

Library of Congress Cataloging in Publication Data

Bowie, Malcolm.

Mallarmé and the art of being difficult.

Bibliography: p.
Includes index.
1. Mallarmé, Stéphane, 1842–1898 – Criticism and interpretation. I. Title.
PQ2344.Z5B6   841'.8   77–82488
ISBN 0 521 21813 6

CONTENTS

Acknowledgements vi

Notes on Texts vii

Prefatory Note viii

1 Difficulty 1

2 'Prose pour des Esseintes' 19

3 *Un Coup de dés jamais n'abolira le hasard* 91

Concluding Note 147

Appendix. The earlier version of 'Prose' 155

Notes 157

List of Works Cited 182

Index 191

v

ACKNOWLEDGEMENTS

I should like to thank all those students at the Universities of East Anglia and Cambridge with whom I've discussed French poetry in recent years for the many stimulating ideas they've given me. My thanks also go to those colleagues who by their questions and counter-arguments made me think again when I read versions of Chapters One and Two to the Cambridge Modern Language Society and the Society for French Studies, and to the following generous friends who've helped me in many ways during the writing of this book: Eva Bron, Roger Cardinal, Christine Crow, Ann Duncan, Alison Finch, Linda Gillman, Sam Hackett, Tim Mathews, Clive Scott, John Taylor, Michael Tilby, Manya Zwalf. I am greatly indebted to Lloyd Austin and Alison Fairlie who read this work in its successive stages, put me on to new lines of enquiry and encouraged me by many acts of kindness. To them both, and to Michael Black, who read the complete manuscript and suggested many ways in which it could be improved, I should like to express my gratitude.

NOTE ON TEXTS

Throughout I have used the first published text of 'Prose pour des Esseintes' (*La Revue indépendante*, t. II, no. 3, jan. 1885, 194–7), although I have suppressed the brackets which originally surrounded the dedication 'pour des Esseintes' and the dash which appeared beneath the second quatrain. Of the few small punctuation-matters in which this text differs from that of the *Œuvres complètes* (ed. Henri Mondor and G. Jean-Aubry, 'Bibliothèque de la Pléiade', Gallimard, 1951, 55–7), only one affects the sense of the poem: there is no contemporary authority for the final comma in 7.3. My text of *Un Coup de dés* is that of the first single-volume edition of the poem (Gallimard, 1914) which is reproduced here by permission of Éditions Gallimard.

PREFATORY NOTE

This is neither an introductory guide to Mallarmé nor a general critical study of his works. It is an attempt to state a problem – that of reading 'the difficult Mallarmé poem' –, to suggest solutions to it and examine in some detail the two works of art, 'Prose pour des Esseintes' and *Un Coup de dés*, which raise that problem in its most acute practical form. It so happens that these seem to me the finest of Mallarmé's works, and one of the incidental things that I shall do in the pages which follow is set forth the grounds for my preference. But I have no wish to urge these works upon my reader as the 'essential Mallarmé' or as the best route towards an understanding of his whole achievement. For Mallarmé is an artist too largely responsive to experience and too versatile in his verbal power to be usefully epitomised in this way. The world revealed to us by Émilie Noulet in her extraordinary pioneering study *L'Œuvre poétique de Stéphane Mallarmé* and by Jean-Pierre Richard in his monumental *L'Univers imaginaire de Mallarmé* is indefinitely rich, complex and surprising. Any reader who still manages to think of Mallarmé as the intense local embodiment of a single attitude or aptitude should read these works without delay. (Newcomers will find a brief and pointed introduction in A. R. Chisholm's *Mallarmé's 'Grand Œuvre'*).

That Mallarmé's work in verse and prose is often exceptionally difficult is the best known, and in many cases the only known, thing about him. Literary chroniclers and critics have responded to this difficulty in a variety of ways: some, for reasons of simple snobbery, have applauded it ('Odi profanum vulgus...'); some have excused it as an unfortunate feature of an otherwise admirable period style; others have seen it as a Blatant Beast which righteousness obliges the critic to pursue, overpower and domesticate; others more propitiating have argued that it is really no cause for alarm and can be dealt with by any reader adequately supplied with good will and glossaries.[1] The most productive views of this difficulty are often to be found as asides in the discussion of individual texts or, in the case of Gardner Davies's excellent essay, as an epilogue to a sequence of exegeses (*Les 'Tombeaux' de Mallarmé*). What follows is an attempt to state and illustrate more sustainedly a positive view of the matter. Throughout I have referred to 'difficulty' rather than to 'obscurity': for although the latter term is sometimes used in the sense I intend (Herbert Read, for example, speaks of 'an obscurity due to the honesty and objectivity of the poet'[2]), it often carries the inappropriate suggestion that clear matter has been wantonly and artificially darkened.

I spoke at the start of 'the difficult Mallarmé poem' as if there were a single underlying poem-type. But Mallarmé's poems are difficult in different ways and at different levels of intensity. Certain of them are difficult to come at, to get meaning from, but yield to pressure. Others are mobile and stubbornly unsmooth patterns of meaning which, while yielding to pressure in some of their parts or aspects, leave us with an abiding residue of unsolved questions. Mallarmé wrote many poems which are semantically uncertain when we first come to them but which allow us during subsequent readings to guess towards a goal. In reading them we travel in the expectation that we will arrive sooner or later at a single main sense for the work – around which other senses, tried and discarded on the way, may or may not, according to our tastes in the matter, be allowed to linger as a suggestive atmosphere. But other poems have difficulty at their centre, being concerned with open metaphysical questions. And the simple asking of these questions becomes in Mallarmé's hands such a powerful means of organising experience that anything short of a celestial solution to them would be flat and uninformative in comparison. Such poems are centred upon difficulties which are the product of an intended and scrupulous indecision on the poet's part.

I shall be devoting most of the discussion which follows to works of this second type, although I hope that much of what I say will be of interest to those whose main preoccupations lie elsewhere in Mallarmé, or in the work of other poets. The poems I have chosen to look at in detail are those in which the difficulties of reading are given their fullest motivation by the inveterately difficult substance on which the poet has chosen to operate. In disappointing many of our familiar notions of coherence and intelligibility, these texts invite us into a world of uncertainty and speculation comparable to that in which the poet's own metaphysical enquiries take place. The trouble we may experience in working out Mallarmé's meanings in these poems is, of course, in several important ways *not* comparable to the trouble he had in deciding what his metaphysical questions and their possible answers were to be. Indeed much of our own trouble has already been taken before we are in a position to know whether questions of this kind are present in the poems at all. I am not suggesting that our struggle to understand 'Prose pour des Esseintes' and *Un Coup de dés* is in itself a philosophical activity, nor that immediately comprehensible poems on the same themes are impossible to envisage. My main contention will be that the speculative states of mind into which Mallarmé's poetic textures cast us provide one singularly rich and emotionally charged context in which to take his philosophical uncertainties seriously, and that our most important collaboration with the poet begins when we ourselves agree to be uncertain.

Although much excellent work has been done on the general interpretation of Mallarmé's poems, their verbal fabric has seldom been examined closely. In the pages which follow I have suggested several ways in which such an examination might proceed and included in my notes to Chapter Two a good deal of information on approaches to poetic language which might usefully be applied to Mallarmé in due course.

CHAPTER ONE

Difficulty

The way in this world is like the edge of a blade. On this side is the underworld, and on that side is the underworld, and the way of life lies between.

HASIDIC SAYING

The idea that poetry may be both pleasurable and difficult is not an invention of the modern age. From the early stages of the European tradition, many poets have absorbed 'difficult' contemporary ideas into their works or given those works an elaborate ground-plan of argument. Lucretius, Dante, Milton, Blake and Hugo, for example, found in the main intellectual currents of their day a source not of ornament but of primary material and informing perspective for their verse. And it is not simply these masters of large-scale poetic design who make nonsense of the commonplace notion that the minds of philosophers are impressively tough and those of poets endearingly tender. For many lyric poets have contrived densely argumentative textures for their verse; many have regarded cryptography as a worthy component of their art and have expected readers to enjoy being ingenious in the decipherment of poetic codes. Consider for a moment the extraordinary hundred-year span of European culture which began in 1540: at the beginning of this period Scève was completing his *Délie* and at the end Marvell was writing his early poems, while in the years between, such masters of serried complexity as Greville, Góngora, Marino and Donne had lived and died.[1] It was the lesson of all these writers – to say nothing of the many lesser talents of the age who flamboyantly built anagrams, name and number symbolisms, acrostics, conundrums, recondite puns and allusions or tightrope-walking allegories into their texts – that the reader's calculating skills could not only find proper employment in the experience of poetry but could at moments positively enhance the quality of his emotional and imaginative response. Difficult poetry is not new, and it has not become more difficult – in the sense of demanding more intellectual work from us – in the last hundred years, although a copious sub-literature of readers' guides, skeleton keys and explicators' manuals is urgently concerned to persuade us otherwise.

But an important change has occurred, and this is not a matter of providing us with tougher codes to crack or more intricate arguments to unravel. The change is far more radical than that and far less easily assimilable to conventional academic techniques of exegesis. We have witnessed a major epistemological upheaval – or a 'paradigm-shift'[2] as many philosophers of science and historians of ideas would nowadays say – for which new explanatory tools have to be made. For in the work of many modern poets difficulty is the very life of the poem; we have been taken from a world in which the decipherer could confidently envisage solutions and anticipate the gratifying sensations of discovery even during the early stages of his quest. The sense of pattern to which we accede by our intellectual and imaginative efforts as readers of 'the modern poem' seldom hardens into a fixed framework of ideas or images. Productive reading entails that patterns be made and willingly broken, tested and revised or discarded. The frame of mind essential to the reader of much modern poetry is that of an experimentalist for whom speculation and hypothesis proceed continuously, *sine die*, and for whom certainty is the remotest and least practical of goals.

Mallarmé occupies a special place in the modern tradition. Among French poets of the nineteenth century he was the most adventurously and the most trenchantly agnostic: his powers of doubt played not only upon the time-honoured theologies and theodicies of Europe, but upon those newer, secular cults of beauty and 'the spirit' of which he is popularly thought to be an uncritical exponent. The arts of tangential thinking and oblique, suggestive utterance that had already flowered so finely in Baudelaire, Nerval and the Hugo of the shorter lyrical works

were brought by Mallarmé to their highest point of refinement
– or of morbid self-indulgence, as his detractors would claim.
But if certain elements of Mallarmé's work clearly develop and
perfect an established post-Romantic mode of thought, others
are quite as clearly modern in their allegiance. What is more,
the writer of the late sonnets, 'Prose pour des Esseintes' and
Un Coup de dés is not at all a mere precursor or apprentice within
the tradition of adamant, open-ended difficulty that I evoked
above. On the contrary his poetry has here too an exemplary
power: in its sensuous complexity, its verbal inventiveness, its
unceasing attack on all that is smoothly commonsensical and
its readiness to run the risk of complete semantic breakdown,
it provides the modern literary temperament with a definitive
portrait of itself.

Mallarmé is incomparably sensitive to those moments in
human experience when familiar meanings dissolve and vacancy,
or a dizzying blur of potential meanings, takes their place. His
most compelling imaginative strokes often portray disruptions
and discontinuities within the operations of mind. Many of his
poems could as usefully be examined for their gaps, elisions,
discrepancies and unannounced shifts of register as for the interplay between their units of sustained sense. Refusing to be
peremptory in his search for coherence, he may suspend an idea
while it is still half-formed in order to explore its constituent
parts or to give cognate or opposed ideas their say in the matter.
I shall argue that this capacity for the manipulation of dramatic
hiatus within his texts is one of Mallarmé's vital strengths as
a thinker.

Here are some examples of ways in which Mallarmé may
introduce these sudden breaks in sense. None of these devices
is peculiar to him, of course; comparable examples could easily
be collected from the works of, say, Hugo or Baudelaire. What is
remarkable is the frequency with which they occur in Mallarmé
and the variety of expressive functions they serve. He may leave
a syntactic pattern incomplete, as at the start of *L'Après-midi d'un
faune*:

Réfléchissons...

> ou si les femmes dont tu gloses
> Figurent un souhait de tes sens fabuleux!
> Faune, l'illusion s'échappe des yeux bleus
> Et froids, comme une source en pleurs, de la plus
>   chaste:[3]

(The whole opening section is remarkable, and not least for the way in which its many such breaks suggest now the desultoriness, now the self-overtaking urgency of sensual appetite.) He may place a smaller complete sentence as an unannounced parenthesis within a larger sentence, as in the sixth of these lines from 'Prose pour des Esseintes':

> L'ère d'autorité se trouble
> Lorsque, sans nul motif, on dit
> De ce midi que notre double
> Inconscience approfondit
>
> Que, sol des cent iris, son site,
> Ils savent s'il a bien été,
> Ne porte pas de nom que cite
> L'or de la trompette d'Été.[4]

or he may allow subordinate material to develop an emotional weight equal to that of the main proposition upon which it depends, as in the middle lines of this quatrain:

> Quand l'ombre menaça de la fatale loi
> Tel vieux Rêve, désir et mal de mes vertèbres,
> Affligé de périr sous les plafonds funèbres
> Il a ployé son aile indubitable en moi.[5]

(At first reading the descriptions 'subordinate' and 'main' are of course difficult to apply to the parts of Mallarmé's sentence; the reader has to work to make the distinction and, before making it, may already have grasped intuitively the main contrasts which it enacts: between fate-governed world and creative self and, within that self, between longing and resignation.)

Or, most frequently of all, he may encourage open conflict between the metrical and semantic patterns of a poem:

> Ses purs ongles très haut dédiant leur onyx,
> L'Angoisse, ce minuit, soutient, lampadophore,
> Maint rêve vespéral brûlé par le Phénix[6]

These are the opening lines of a sonnet quite unmatched in its linguistic *bravura*. Here, and in the remainder of the text, the integrity of the alexandrine as a semantic unit is by turns affirmed (lines 1,3) and violently denied (line 2). The first line is a complete suspended clause, rather like an ablative absolute in Latin; the third is a self-contained noun phrase providing 'soutient' with its object. But even after several readings the second line is likely to leave the reader in mental disarray. For although the rhythm and the sound-pattern of the line give it an immediate, almost formulaic, authority, it is the start of a proposition which will not be complete until the fifth line of the poem. And the line is not only removed by metre from its syntactic dependents but composed of sub-units which are themselves cut off from each other. The four ideas do not unfold as a continuous syntactic sequence, but are free to develop new relationships of affinity or contrast among themselves: 'ce minuit' is strictly an adverbial phrase, but it makes poignant sense if it is read as being in apposition to 'L'Angoisse'; 'lampadophore' is strictly in apposition to 'L'Angoisse', but it has a neat paradoxical thrust to it if read as a reference back to 'ce minuit'. Mallarmé has manipulated his syntax in such a way as to allow and encourage his reader to make these subsidiary metonymic connections within the line, and see anguish as a kind of midnight and midnight as a source of illumination.

An even more rapid *staccato* is present in phrases like the following from 'Hommage' (to Wagner):

> Du souriant fracas originel haï[7]

The characteristic problem here is twofold. The noun and its adjectives together form an astonishingly improbable sequence: as we move from word to word we are obliged to leap the wide gaps which separate their fields of association – to leap from the physical to the moral, from the spatial to the temporal, from the outward to the inward. At each word-boundary we have to re-think our previous route and make new guesses at the way ahead. But in addition the syntax is ambiguous (does the line mean 'haï du souriant fracas originel'? is the preposition a simple indication of place or origin? or an equivalent of 'depuis', to be answered in the 'jusque' of the next line but one?[8]), and each new scansion of this syntax will bring new kinds of relationship between the four ideas into play. Syntactic ambiguity gives each member of improbable word-chains such as this an unusual independence and immediacy: each word is a gravitational centre around which possible meanings of the entire sentence gather. These virtualities will of course become fewer as we move towards a relatively stable syntactic armature for the poem. But the meanings we relinquish do not simply disappear: the atmosphere of multiple potentiality which they create is part of Mallarmé's poetic substance.

Discontinuities such as those I have listed are a prime source both of difficulty and of suggestive richness. The double effort required to allow Mallarmé's gaps their full disjunctive and destructive power, yet at the same time remain attentive to the multitude of invisible currents which pass back and forth between the separated segments, will strike many readers as inexcusably arduous and unrewarding. The view I shall propose is that such moments are of the essence in Mallarmé and that time spent learning to read them is amply repaid.

The objects with which this self-fracturing discourse confronts us are multiple and inconstant: as we read a further word or phrase within a poem, an object may change its shape, or its meaning, or cease to have a meaning, or cease to be there at all. There are two distinct and well-tried ways of envisaging the Mallarmé world-picture and of giving due prominence within it to these cessations and evaporations. Many of Mallarmé's most devoted readers belong, according to which of these ways they adopt, to one of two sullenly uncommunicating clans. For the one group, Mallarmé's world is essentially that of the middle-class domestic interior. There is a comfortable clutter about the place: trinkets, mementoes, books, musical instruments, fans and looking-glasses gently punctuate a tranquil, habitable space. The poet's clairvoyant eye is not of course to be duped by the solid surface of these things: he sees how fragile they all are, how readily subject to collapse and decay, how vulnerable to the dissolving touch of thought. But he has his safeguards: the vacuum left by a familiar object as it disappears is soon filled by others of the same sort; the elemental swirl of the night sky is framed and tamed by the drawing-room window. Parts of the customary décor may be erased, but as a general presence it remains and protects. For the other group, however, Mallarmé is a metaphysical adventurer, 'voyaging through strange seas of thought, alone'. His world is beyond substance, such objects as it contains being the merest vestiges, vacant and transparent, from a forgotten age of sensuous illusion. There is nothing comforting about this realm. The joys and disasters to be found there are extravagantly un-domestic: when a sense of metaphysical nullity comes upon the poet it is absolute, all-consuming and unanswerable; when this sense loses its grip upon him and transcendent purity is shown forth, his idealist yearning is completely and ecstatically fulfilled. Both these scenarios are useful – it is convenient, after all, to carry a problem-filled world around in symmetrical, capsule form – and both seriously diminish the subtlety and versatility of Mallarmé's mind.[9]

A natural enough tendency when faced with the intellectual challenge of a poem as complex as the following is to confine it within a unitary scheme, to straighten out all its odd corners and to answer the question 'what does this mean?' with panic-stricken rapidity:

Le vierge, le vivace et le bel aujourd'hui
Va-t-il nous déchirer avec un coup d'aile ivre
Ce lac dur oublié que hante sous le givre
Le transparent glacier des vols qui n'ont pas fui!

Un cygne d'autrefois se souvient que c'est lui
Magnifique mais qui sans espoir se délivre

Pour n'avoir pas chanté la région où vivre
Quand du stérile hiver a resplendi l'ennui.

Tout son col secouera cette blanche agonie
Par l'espace infligée à l'oiseau qui le nie,
Mais non l'horreur du sol où le plumage est pris.

Fantôme qu'à ce lieu son pur éclat assigne,
Il s'immobilise au songe froid de mépris
Que vêt parmi l'exil inutile le Cygne.[10]

The poem is so arresting and intricate as a pattern of sounds
that many readers will spend a long time speaking it, or re-
hearsing it upon the inward ear, before seeking to acquire anything more than a minimum supporting drift of sense. Problems
begin when the sense is thought about in detail. The usual
defensive reaction to the poem at this stage is to make it into a
picture – by ignoring or minimising its abundant abstractions
and stressing the visual appeal of certain images – and to
superimpose upon the picture a simple allegorical grid: the
swan is the poet, the ice which traps it his sense of impotence
as an artist, the dawning day his long-awaited inspiration, and
so forth. But how dull the poem becomes when tidied up and
rigidified in this way. How many eccentricities and paradoxes
have to be swept aside in order to keep the allegory intact. The
first quatrain, for example, is alive with problematic implications. The trapped creature (as yet unspecified) is not simply in
opposition to its captor, but has an intimate affinity with it:
the bird's 'unflown flights' are ice within ice. Similarly the day
which is invoked by the creature as an external liberating force
is expected to intervene with a perfectly creaturely gesture
('avec un coup d'aile ivre'). Flights unflown are not flights;
stillness is complete. Yet within its casing the creature already
has the mobility of a haunting spirit. Even the order of the
words has its tricks to play: we have read seven words of the
poem before we are able to know that a male virgin and a male
sprite are not among the characters in the drama. But by the
time 'vierge' and 'vivace' have assumed their rightful status as
adjectives (and not adjectival nouns), these phantom presences

have already appeared on the stage. In the same way, we must wait until the third line before being told that 'nous' is the indirect and not the direct object of 'déchirer': in the hypothesis he makes, the subject of this interior monologue is first torn and then the mere witness of tearing.

Several of the crucial questions of identity raised in this quatrain remain unsolved throughout the poem. The swan is by turns painfully separate from its surroundings and radiantly continuous and consubstantial with them. In the first tercet the bird is the unwilling receiver of a whiteness thrust upon it from without, while in the second it takes its place in the world by virtue of a whiteness from within itself. Moreover the attitudes of the swan *persona* to its imprisoned state are presented in two contrary, interwoven strains. Removed from its context and simplified, one of these strains would run: the trapped swan is despairing and self-reproachful for having failed, at the onset of winter, in its responsibilities as singer and harbinger; it rises in pain and protest against its sterile oppressor, but in the end succumbs and resignedly acknowledges its own sterility. The other, however, would run: the trapped swan is magnificent, its prison resplendent; in captivity it has acquired a pure spiritual energy which it willingly contains and subdues; exile is its badge of honour, allowing it to achieve perfect self-mastery and placing it at a far and fortunate remove from the contingent world of practical endeavour. Until the last line each of these distinct attitudes is expounded in its own distinctive set of words. But there the two attitudes merge in the completely equivocal 'inutile'. The word clearly refers us back to previous notions of barrenness and immobility; but for Mallarmé, no less than for Gautier in his manifestoes of aestheticism, the notion of utility as applied to matters of the spirit is scandalous and repugnant: to be 'inutile' is to be happily released from the pursuit of utilitarian goals.

I do not wish to suggest that the pictorial elements of the poem are unimportant. But they are less important in themselves than in their quick, cross-cutting relationship with the poet's array of conceptual terms. For whereas the visible scene is one of complete stasis – such actions as might engage the eye are confined to a conjectural future (lines 2,9) – the invisible inner world which interrupts it is tumultous, contradictory and self-correcting. The constant interplay between the two planes is exquisitely resolved in the phrase 'Il s'immobilise' (line 13): the already stationary bird 'makes itself stationary' in the sense that it is now prepared to suspend its powers of spectral movement, allow inner state to mimic outer state and adopt by personal volition what had previously been enforced by impersonal circumstance.

The poem contains a host of further peculiarities which I shall not comment upon here. What is remarkable is that Mallarmé's contradictions, his formidable art of suggestion and counter-suggestion, leave not the slightest impression of scrappy, indecisive thinking: there are no sonorous trivia in the text; no metaphors which, promising much, provide little; no philosophical issues summoned up simply for intellectual ostentation. Mallarmé's discontinuous discourse – his disruption of conventional word-order, his rapid oscillation between notions and images, or between past, present and future time-levels – produces an intensive pattern of cross-reference between the parts of the poem. There is a clear danger here: that the poet in cultivating such discontinuity will too thoroughly liberate his words from the local relationships which their place in a syntactic sequence dictates, and provide a confusing surfeit of alternative connections. But however disruptive the text, it never becomes an asyntactic haze: it is organised in such a way that the reader is given guidance in his connection-making by a strong framework of recurrent analogies and oppositions. These act as models of economical structure and help us to keep order among the incidental messages which emanate from the text as we read.

The elements of the poem are so flexible in their capacity for combination and re-combination, and the whole thing is so richly productive as a sense-making system, that readers who seek for complete watertightness in their interpretations are likely to remain baffled or take refuge in allegory. There are no grounds whatever for reading the poem as 'really' an account of the private tribulations of the poet, or of creative artists at large. It has to do with song – or with expressive utterance in general – and to that extent 'the Poet' is an implied presence. But he is not present in order to ensure that botanists, bus-conductors or corn-chandlers are excluded. For the poem opens out flickeringly upon a set of basic existential dilemmas: to move or to be still; to rebel or to acquiesce; to remain the same or to change by moral self-scrutiny; to strive for individuality or to dissolve oneself within larger metaphysical entities. And these awesome generalities are checked, kept in focus and given delicate gradations of sensuous appeal by a single complex image: the image not of a poet with the emblems of his craft, but of the white plumes and muscular neck of an ice-bound swan. This is where Mallarmé begins from, and where his finely differentiated debate finds its equilibrium.

Problems of the same kind arise even more acutely in reading and thinking about the work which many admirers of Mallarmé would argue is his finest single achievement: 'Prose pour des Esseintes'. My next chapter is devoted to an extended account of this poem. But certain preliminary remarks are relevant here. 'Prose' is so daunting in its complexity that the reader has no choice but to simplify and schematise if he is to make headway at all. What seems to me unfortunate is that the means chosen for making the poem more comprehensible should so often lead to the creation of a false smoothness and sequentiality. Much has been made, for example, of its quasi-liturgical elements and its general atmosphere of ritual. The poem has been seen as a gradually unfolding hymn to the Ideal and to the potency of poetic language. In this view the poem is difficult because obscure and obscure because oracular utterances are tradition-ally so, being calculated to confound those who show them-selves by their stupidity, flippancy or clay-footedness to be unworthy of initiation into the higher mysteries; the difficulty of the poem is of the sort which is produced when a simple underlying message appears in a heavily disguised and orna-mented form.

But the poem is not continuous either as argument or as story, and not continuously or even mainly hymn-like. The central episode (quatrains 6–9), beginning

> Oui, dans une île que l'air charge
> De vue et non de visions
> Toute fleur s'étalait plus large
> Sans que nous en devisions.

in which the Idea-flowers appear before the poet and his companion, is preceded and followed by passages of anxious debate. These are quatrains 4–5 which begin

> L'ère d'autorité se trouble

and quatrains 10–12 which begin

> Oh ! sache l'Esprit de litige,

The phrases 'L'ère d'autorité' and 'l'Esprit de litige' both introduce into the poem the voice of doubt, speaking on behalf of philosophical scepticism or of truculent common sense.[11] The existence of the Ideal realm and the truth of the poet's report are shown to be open to dispute. But Mallarmé does not hold the carpers at a distance and simply concede to them by incorporating certain of their objections and *caveats* into the texture of his poem. Doubt is given its full dignity and disruptive weight: the syntax of these quatrains is fragmented, within qualifications further qualifications appear, and the propositions which contain the poet's own creed are invaded and contaminated by their contradictories. What is elsewhere announced as unarguable certainty is re-examined in these quatrains from a rigorously sceptical viewpoint. And between refusal and acceptance of the poet's claims no intermediate ground of politely reserved judgment is proposed. The conceptual breaks between these three central sections are complete, and reinforced on both occasions by simultaneous metrical and syntactic breaks.

The large and abrupt contradiction which is thus installed in the middle of 'Prose' cannot be conveniently smoothed away.

If, however, we abandon any hasty attempt to make the poem homogeneous and if we pay due attention to this contradiction, we can see that it is but the most manifest and architecturally the most impressive instance of a persistent tendency within Mallarmé's thinking in this work. Here are two further examples from among many: the Ideal realm appears in the poem now as a grace, a gift unasked for, a miracle of spontaneous and unmediated perception, now as the goal of concentrated and painstaking intellectual effort; in the quest for the Ideal, language appears now as an irrelevance, or, what is worse, a sign of imperfect faith, now as the supreme creative instrument. The unity we are able to envisage when we register and retain these discontinuities, rather than smuggle them out of the text in order to preserve our everyday expectations of intelligibility, is again, as in the case of 'Le vierge, le vivace...', a difficult unity – the product not of a uniform and fluently articulated argument but of a whole pattern of internal oppositions and tensions. Mallarmé's is a world in which nothing is self-evident enough to be a premise or logically demonstrable enough to be a conclusion. The stages of argument which we would usually expect to find leading one to the next in a linear sequence are, in these poems, all in force at the same time. Thinking proceeds by the reciprocal definition of contrary states and statements.

I hope these brief remarks have shown that the difficulty of Mallarmé's major poems, far from being an encumbrance, is a positive factor in their power as imaginative constructions. The abrupt internal differences which are packed tightly into a Mallarmé text may be thought of as a kind of counter-entropy: by his refusal of smoothness, his setting up within the text of many more boundaries and barriers than are necessary for the transmission of simple, cogent propositions, the poet ensures that his poem is a rich and compact store of information. But fruitful reading involves much more than the efficient retrieval of the information that the poet has found such an ingenious and economical way of storing. For in these barrier-laden texts ideas develop an impulsive life of their own: they form sudden, improbable alliances; they are intersected or pulled out of shape by their neighbours; part-ideas merge into unpredictable wholes. The complex segmentation of the text gives it a capacity to release much more sense than any one reading can encompass: it stands as a permanent invitation to further thought, addressed to those readers who have available the necessary patience, curiosity and intellectual energy.

But to be patient, curious and intellectually energetic is not enough. Much of what I have said might suggest that this is a poetry designed solely for those who take an acute delight in the operations of their own intelligence and in observing similar operations in others. The ideal Mallarmé reader as I have sketched him so far may have emerged (although I hope not) as a dilettante of the intellect, a compulsive weaver of intricate and trivial mental tapestry. Mallarmé certainly expects his reader to have a developed speculative skill and to be able to take pleasure in long moments of imaginative suspense during which an awaited resolution is tantalisingly deferred. But he does not make things easy for the appropriately endowed reader by allowing him to remain serenely detached while his speculations proceed. For the surface of the poems is so aggressively fragmented that even the most accomplished reader runs the risk of finding no more than superior nonsense as the reward for his endeavours.

Mallarmé is the type of the modern artist as portrayed by Anton Ehrenzweig in his brilliant study of the creative imagination, *The Hidden Order of Art*[12] – the artist, that is to say, who is intent upon breaking up ready-made *Gestalten* and smooth surface textures in order to compel his audience to look elsewhere for artistic coherence, to venture beneath the surface into the difficult, undifferentiated world of unconscious process, to interrupt the easy flow of horizontal perception with strenuous excursions into multi-level, all-at-once 'verticality'.[13] By the constant severing, meshing and overlapping of his dominant ideas, Mallarmé runs counter to many of our cherished habits as verbal performers. So much of the time we spend in talking or writing is devoted to maintaining a pleasant continuity of discourse – people as different from each other as the epic poet, the orator, the ratiocinator and the prattler would all agree that such continuity is a worthwhile goal – that we may find ourselves upset and indignant at these studiously disjointed texts. Mallarmé makes us think again about the directions in which artistic coherence may be pursued and the verbal methods by which it may be articulated. He invites us to take risks. He exposes us to a special kind of anxiety by making it extremely hard for us to extract an idea from a text in a simple, manageable form: we are forced to leave it where it was, hedged about and baffled by its cognates, collaterals and contraries. What at one moment can seem a compressed and richly interfused set of meanings can the next seem a frightening turmoil of disconnected scraps.

This is the sign of a deep-rooted and essential paradox in Mallarmé's work, and one with which I shall be much concerned in later pages of this study. The discontinuity which I have described at length is a treacherous ally. On the one hand it is a technical necessity in poems which reflect the complex multi-dimensional creativity of mind. Mallarmé's exceptional skill and versatility in the manipulation of hiatus separate him once and for all from the one-problem/one-answer techniques of cryptography. Each of his great poems presents the provisional results of an intellectual and emotional experiment and, at the same time, a portrait of the characteristic quandaries and defeats of the experimental process: the poet by interrupting his crucial acts of thought leaves the reader with much further thinking to perform and incorporates the sensations of mental struggle into his finished work. But on the other hand this same discontinuity, when used as frequently and variously as Mallarmé uses it, has a different and cumulatively more sinister power. For it is all-pervasive: it does not single out shoddy thoughts for interruption and allow momentous ones to proceed unhindered; it reminds us insistently that all thinking is temporary and that all knowledge has limits. Yet this is far from being a kindly, conventional reminder that quests for intelligibility can take place only within the unintelligible, that knowledge is necessarily achieved and defined within a resistant medium. For Mallarmé the best thought is that which most scrupulously acknowledges its own frailty; and the more scrupulous the thought becomes the thinner the partition which separates it from total vacuity. Looked at in this way, the difficulty of the difficult poem is the mind's hesitation, its incredulity, its panic when faced with supreme, nullifying simplicity.

CHAPTER TWO

'Prose pour des Esseintes'

The structure is now visible; what is inchoate is here stated; we are not so various or so mean; we have made oblongs and stood them upon squares. This is our triumph; this is our consolation.
VIRGINIA WOOLF: *The Waves*

PROSE
pour des Esseintes

1

Hyperbole! de ma mémoire
Triomphalement ne sais-tu
Te lever, aujourd'hui grimoire
Dans un livre de fer vêtu :

2

Car j'installe, par la science,
L'hymne des cœurs spirituels
En l'œuvre de ma patience,
Atlas, herbiers et rituels.

3

Nous promenions notre visage
(Nous fûmes deux, je le maintiens)
Sur maints charmes de paysage,
O sœur, y comparant les tiens.

4

L'ère d'autorité se trouble
Lorsque, sans nul motif, on dit
De ce midi que notre double
Inconscience approfondit

5

Que, sol des cent iris, son site,
Ils savent s'il a bien été,
Ne porte pas de nom que cite
L'or de la trompette d'Été.

6
Oui, dans une île que l'air charge
De vue et non de visions
Toute fleur s'étalait plus large
Sans que nous en devisions.

7
Telles, immenses, que chacune
Ordinairement se para
D'un lucide contour, lacune
Qui des jardins la sépara.

8
Gloire du long désir, Idées,
Tout en moi s'exaltait de voir
La famille des iridées
Surgir à ce nouveau devoir,

9
Mais cette sœur sensée et tendre
Ne porta son regard plus loin
Que sourire et, comme à l'entendre
J'occupe mon antique soin.

10
Oh! sache l'Esprit de litige,
A cette heure où nous nous taisons,
Que de lis multiples la tige
Grandissait trop pour nos raisons,

11
Et non comme pleure la rive
Quand son jeu monotone ment
A vouloir que l'ampleur arrive
Parmi mon jeune étonnement

12
D'ouïr tout le Ciel et la carte
Sans fin attestés sur mes pas,
Par le flot même qui s'écarte,
Que ce pays n'exista pas.

13
L'enfant abdique son extase
Et docte déjà par chemins
Elle dit le mot: Anastase!
Né pour d'éternels parchemins,

14
Avant qu'un sépulcre ne rie
Sous aucun climat, son aïeul,
De porter ce nom: Pulchérie!
Caché par le trop grand glaïeul.

I

At the beginning of *Le Côté de Guermantes* Proust's narrator asks, in one of those sudden subsidiary reflections in which the novel abounds: 'N'est-ce pas déjà un premier élément de complexité ordonnée, de beauté, quand en entendant une rime, c'est-à-dire quelque chose qui est à la fois pareil et autre que la rime précédente, qui est motivé par elle, mais y introduit la variation d'une idée nouvelle, on sent deux systèmes qui se superposent, l'un de pensée, l'autre de métrique?'[1] The originality of La Berma among actresses, he goes on to say, lay in her extraordinary ability to superimpose upon these components of the dramatic text a third system of expressive vocal gesture. But as a mere stage on the way towards a definition of the actor's art, Proust has here stated with remarkable clarity a central feature of the poet's. For Valéry the same double nature of poetic compositions was a cherished theme and the subject of much fine meditative writing:

> Il est étrange que l'on s'évertue à former un discours
> qui doive observer des conditions simultanées

parfaitement hétéroclites : *musicales, rationnelles, significatives, suggestives,* et qui exigent une liaison suivie ou entretenue entre un rythme et une syntaxe, entre le *son* et le *sens* [. . .] il y a un langage poétique dans lequel les mots ne sont plus les mots de l'usage pratique et libre. Ils ne s'associent plus selon les mêmes attractions ; ils sont chargés de deux valeurs simultanément engagées et d'importance équivalente : leur son et leur effet psychique instantané. Ils font songer alors à ces nombres complexes des géomètres, et l'accouplement de la *variable phonétique* avec la *variable sémantique* engendre des problèmes de prolongement et de convergence que les poètes résolvent les yeux bandés. . .[2]

Both Proust and Valéry depart significantly from a traditional view of how poetic language works. Those verse-elements which Aristotle and generations of later writers on poetry had seen as 'pleasurable accessories'[3] to the business of verbal representation are now held to have a system of their own, and to demand a skilled duplicity of poet and reader alike. Sound-system and sense-system are heterogeneous, and the mystical echoes which many nineteenth-century writers had heard travelling between them, and suggesting the existence between them of some unfathomable kinship, are heard no more. The relations between the two systems are now a source of intellectual tension and excitement.

But despite the commonplaceness today of this general assumption, the analysis of the ways in which the two systems are related in specific works of poetry remains a backward science. There are two main reasons for this: first, critics have been conscious of how easy it is to mistake features of one's private response for features of the text under discussion and, in the words of Dr Johnson's pungent warning on the subject, improperly to 'ascribe to the numbers the effects of the sense'.[4] Secondly, it is a matter of some convenience to assume that if verse-elements emerge at all into the foreground of the reader's attention they do so merely to confirm the general tone and direction of the work, or to adorn its principal messages. To be expressive, in this view, is simply to say the same thing twice, using two different, superimposed codes. I do not wish to suggest that this supposition is wrong. Indeed if it is to be judged by its yield of useful commentary it is the single most profitable account of the relationship between sense and 'numbers'. Such monuments as Maurice Grammont's *Le Vers français*[5] have it as their sole theoretical foundation. But it is all too easy to envisage the art of the poet as a single matching activity of mind, at work simultaneously upon sound and sense, and to imagine that in cases where no mutually confirming relationship between the two systems is to be observed, no relationship exists. In the pages which follow, I shall show how various and, on occasion, how eccentric are the ways in which the two systems interact. The rigid 'expressivist' approach to the explanation of poetic effect – which often amounts to a search for ever more rarefied forms of onomatopœia and 'sound symbolism' – has played havoc with many of Mallarmé's poems. The metaphysical desolation of repeated short vowels, the nervous anxiety of feminine rhymes, the stoic resignation of fricatives...criticism is, alas, still encumbered with such consoling fictions.[6] I hope to show that Mallarmé's handling of verse-form, and of the phonetic substance of words, is more subtle and more difficult than this view can ever allow. I am conscious that the later poems of Mallarmé are, by their sheer wealth of poetic artifice, an exceptionally favourable proving-ground for the counter-proposals I shall offer. But I hope that certain readers may feel encouraged by what I write to re-examine, in poets who lend themselves less obviously to such analysis, the relations between thought and metrics, between the phonetic and semantic variables of which poems are made.

II

In 'Prose pour des Esseintes' Mallarmé has brought together two of the grandest and longest-lived themes in the history of Western thought. As so much has been written about the work simply as a local embodiment of Symbolist aesthetic theory, a few words on this larger background may be useful. The first theme is that cleavage between 'otherworldliness' and 'this-worldliness' which Arthur O. Lovejoy saw as the 'primary antithesis in philosophical or religious tendencies'.[7] Mallarmé is here concerned with the existence or not of a supremely real world which overarches the contingent, humdrum realm of sensory appearance and mental reflection. In order to evoke the broad current of thought and feeling in which Mallarmé's poem participates, I cannot do better than quote further from Lovejoy's elegant and imaginative account:

> That other realm, though to those enmeshed in matter, occupied with things of sense, busy with plans of action, or absorbed in personal affections, it appears cold and tenuous and barren of interest and delight, is, to those who have been emancipated through reflection or emotional disillusionment, the final goal of the philosophic quest and the sole region in which either the intellect or the heart of man, ceasing, even in this present life, to pursue shadows, can find rest.[8]

But the familiar accents of otherworldly thinking, and of Platonic idealism in particular, that may be heard in the poem, nowhere have the force of unassailable creed or dogma. The mood of 'Prose pour des Esseintes' is by turns exalted and quizzical, and the great metaphysical question which it reformulates is kept alive throughout by a delicate pattern of assertions and reiterated doubts.[9]

The second theme is concerned with the status of the work of art. Although this theme will be thought by many to have a more distinctively modern ring – internal self-appraisal having become a distinguishing feature of so much twentieth-century art and literature – it is of course no less a 'footnote to Plato' than the first. Once the realm of Ideas is held to exist, and to be the highest if not the sole source of value, works of art come under suspicion. For all works of art, including such verbal compositions as may specifically urge their readers or hearers towards the contemplation of the Ideas, originate in the things of sense and make their appeal to the lower faculties of mind which are equipped to manipulate and organise those things. In his attack on the representative artist in Book X of the *Republic*, Socrates castigates him as the imitator of imitations: in creating works of art he places himself and others who attend to his productions at a third remove from truth.[10]

Although the full severity of Plato's charge is not echoed in the poem, Mallarmé's doubts about the artistic enterprise correspond remarkably closely to the same charge as commuted by neo-Platonism. According to Plotinus, for example, true beauty is to be found only in the intelligible world. But certain elements of the sensible world may share in the creative potency which emanates from the ideal forms, and may have about them a provisional, intermediate beauty, as it were. Plotinus urges man not to be detained by the beauties available to sense, by these mere reflections of the divine realm, but to prepare himself to contemplate that realm directly. And the proper readiness for such contemplation lies not in creative striving but in stillness and silence.[11] In 'Prose pour des Esseintes' the immediate, ecstatic perception of the Ideas is set against the slow indirectness by which the mind carries out its tasks of invention or imitation. At the two points in the poem where the idealist goal is most passionately affirmed the usefulness of verbal articulation in achieving that goal is firmly denied (6.4, 10.2). Elsewhere in the poem the creative capacity of words is proclaimed; and by a simple twist of argument Mallarmé's celebration of language is founded upon the same moral supposition as his critique: that if the Ideas exist, then fidelity to them is the supreme goal of human conduct.

Later in this chapter[12] I shall suggest several further and until now neglected ways in which 'Prose' may be thought of as a Platonic poem. But at this preliminary stage in my enquiry, a third Platonic theme should be mentioned, if only because certain commentators on the poem have found it peculiarly seductive.[13] This is the doctrine of Recollection. This doctrine as expounded by Plato in the *Meno* (80E–86C), the *Phaedrus* (249C) and the *Phaedo* (72E–77A) holds that learning is not the acquisition of new knowledge, but a partial recapturing of the knowledge which the soul of each human being enjoyed in its bodiless, pre-natal existence.[14] In the *Phaedo* it appears as one of three complementary arguments for the immortality of the soul. I am able to find no trace of this or any comparable theory in Mallarmé's poem. Two notions which the poem does contain, and which together seem to have given rise to the misunderstanding, are *memory* (1.1–1.4) and *privileged childhood perception* (which is directly present in 13.1 and indirectly present elsewhere by virtue of the implied identity of the 'enfant' and the 'sœur'). At the start of the poem memory provides the poet with the mass of sensory particulars from which a knowledge of the general forms or classes of things may be extracted,[15] such knowledge being the foundation of his poetic 'science' (2.1). A kindred idea is to be found in Plato, although it is in no way peculiar to him: in the *Euthyphro*, for example, Socrates invites his interlocutor to work out, from the individual cases of pious behaviour which he has come upon, that quality of piety which all such behaviour shares (6D–7E and *passim*); in the *Symposium* Diotima describes the mind's ascent towards absolute Beauty from the local instances of beauty which are available to it through the senses (210ff.). But this is not the doctrine of Recollection; nor is it readily consonant with that doctrine.[16]

As for the second notion I mentioned above, this takes us even further from Mallarmé's alleged Platonic source. Mallarmé suggests that childlike intuition is better equipped than reflective adult intelligence to apprehend the Ideas, and in so doing introduces what to Plato would have seemed a mere frivolity into his account of the transcendent realm. But nowhere in the poem does Mallarmé imply that the superior perceptiveness of the child is to be explained by reference to the advantaged position that it occupies in time: the child is perfectly attuned to the Ideas, but not because it is chronologically closer than the adult to some spiritual pre-existence. Even if an explanation of this sort had been offered the poem would not thereby have been brought into line with Plato's doctrine. For Plato incarnation was a definitive change of state and marked a loss of direct contact with reality. That loss was instantaneous and not progressive: the idea that childhood might be a period of temporary reprieve, a gradually dimming afterglow of transcendent perception, plays no part at all in his account of Recollection. Proponents of the sentimental myth of childhood find it easy of course to annex pre-existence and Recollection as embellishments for their theme. Wordsworth does so in his 'Immortality' Ode:

> Our birth is but a sleep and a forgetting:
> The Soul that rises with us, our life's Star,
> Hath had elsewhere its setting,
> And cometh from afar:
> Not in entire forgetfulness,
> And not in utter nakedness,
> But trailing clouds of glory do we come
> From God, who is our home:
> Heaven lies about us in our infancy![17]

But Mallarmé does not make a connection of this kind; and nothing that he says either about memory or about childlike seeing empowers us to invent one.

My remarks on Plato and neo-Platonism are not intended as a contribution to Mallarmé's intellectual biography. What we find in 'Prose' is a group of ideas which are interestingly similar in structure to ideas launched by Plato and kept alive and under review by the Platonic tradition. But we can scarcely assume from this that Mallarmé was well acquainted with Plato's works or directly influenced by him in writing the poem.[18] The major influences upon the poet at the time when his personal brand of idealism was being formed were unquestionably Baudelaire and Poe, and his fondness for terms such as 'l'Absolu' and 'le Néant' would suggest that Hegelianism – as a provider of philosophical attitudes and jargon if not of developed conceptual models – also played a significant part.[19] My point is simply that Mallarmé's thinking on the

Ideal in 'Prose' is worked out in such a way that it bears a far greater resemblance to the Platonic paradigm than to these other, better publicised, 'sources'. Such a contact is in no way surprising. Indeed Plato's philosophy has proved so durable, and so widely transmissible and assimilable at second hand, that the surprising outcome would be rather that an instance of 'otherworldly' thought in Europe, reaching a certain degree of complexity and self-consciousness, should *fail* to overlap with it.

I have had a practical reason for dwelling at some length upon this classical background. For we shall avoid certain headaches if we remember that important elements of the poet's argument are of an entirely traditional kind, and that he situates his ironic reservations and his heresies within a known framework of debate: it is because Mallarmé draws thus upon a shared intellectual heritage that he is entitled to proceed by allusion rather than statement, and to construct around his inherited themes a complex pattern of additional enquiry.

One thing must be made clear. Mallarmé was not a philosopher. He had ideas; they mattered to him. Those ideas which found their way into his poems are discussable in their own right, and there is little excuse for mismanaging them. But when they are artificially codified and separated from the poetic textures in which they are presented to us, little or no originality can be claimed for them. Poems are not ideas-in-dilution, but the products of an independent mode of thought in which feelings, sensations and ideas matter equally and potentiate one another. This was a discovery that Mallarmé made early in his career and never had occasion to revoke. Here, from a letter to Eugène Lefébure, is the integrative action of poetic intelligence magnificently described:

> Je crois que pour être bien l'homme, la nature en pensant, il faut penser de tout son corps, ce qui donne une pensée pleine et à l'unisson comme ces cordes de violon vibrant immédiatement avec sa boîte de bois creux. Les pensées partant du seul cerveau (dont j'ai tant abusé l'été dernier et une

partie de cet hiver) me font maintenant l'effet d'airs
joués sur la partie aiguë de la chanterelle dont le son
ne réconforte pas dans la boîte, – qui passent et s'en
vont sans se *créer*, sans laisser de traces d'elles.[20]

It is this 'whole-body' thinking that the poet invites us in reading him to perform. The detours and dissections of critical
analysis are justified only in so far as they help us to understand
that thinking better and to return better equipped to meet its
challenge.

III

In my discussion of 'Le vierge, le vivace...' in Chapter One, I
tried to suggest some of the sensations and some of the perplexities which await us when we approach the poem for the first
time. While giving my brief portrait of the disorderly early
impressions from which a coherent 'reading' might eventually
arise, I alluded only marginally to the extensive critical literature on the sonnet. My approach to 'Prose' will be different. As
my discussion of the poem proceeds, I shall mention many of
the difficulties early and late which the text creates for the reader
and say a good deal about the practical ways in which the
sense of the work may be won from the words on the page. But
I shall not *begin* with a reconstruction of the reader's initial
gropings for sense. My reasons for not doing so are ones of
economy. For I intend to examine closely the verbal fabric of
the poem and to draw my reader's attention to certain of its
neglected riches; and I have assumed that this could best be
done by establishing at an early stage a fairly firm base from
which to explore. I shall therefore begin by saying briefly what
I consider the general argument of 'Prose' to be, and leave until
later in my analysis the task of describing the ways in which we
may find that argument enhanced, reduplicated, contradicted or
lost from view during the act of reading.

In compiling the outline which follows, I shall rely heavily
upon the work of previous writers and add no more than a suggestion or two of my own to the copious interpretative work

which has already been done. In three articles L. J. Austin has provided much information of outstanding interest and developed a persuasive and comprehensive critical account of the poem.[21] In the first of these articles he reviews all the major readings of the poem which appeared in the period 1886–1953.[22] Daniel Boulay's short monograph *L'Obscurité esthétique de Mallarmé et la 'Prose pour des Esseintes'*[23] is also of particular value. For Austin and Boulay the overall movement of Mallarmé's thought is clear. But rather than impose upon the poem a rigid allegorical frame, both authors seek in discussing points of detail to embrace as many probable readings as may co-exist in harmony. Jean-Pierre Richard writes about the poem in a few characteristically perspicacious pages of *L'Univers imaginaire de Mallarmé*.[24] Georges Poulet's account in *Les Métamorphoses du cercle*[25] differs from the best of the earlier readings not so much in its outline of Mallarmé's thought as in the degree of speculative generalisation which the critic allows himself at each stage of his exposition. Although Poulet is sometimes perfunctory in his observation of textual detail, he reconstructs with unusual insight the interplay between psychological and metaphysical frames of reference within the poem. The most recent review of criticism is to be found in J. P. Verhoeff's article 'Anciens et modernes devant la "Prose pour des Esseintes"'.[26]

The main risk I shall run in giving my own synopsis is that of seeming to state and solve a number of main problems all in a single breath and of producing a premature sense of closure in my reader's mind. Although it suits the purposes of my book to present the poem first of all in paraphrased form, I am conscious that my reading is a provisional one; much of what I say in the later part of this chapter will show the extent to which the questions are still open, and show why it is important for them to remain so. Seasoned explorers of the poem may well find my summary tedious. Newcomers may demur at being offered a broad, schematic account of the text before being shown the details. Both kinds of reader are invited to proceed at once to the next section (p. 37).

The first two quatrains are a self-contained introduction. The main 'narrative' section of the poem begins in the third quatrain and continues until the end of the ninth. Quatrains 10–12 are an apostrophe to 'l'Esprit de litige'; they prolong yet at the same time summarise and comment upon the preceding narrative. The last two quatrains are in the manner of an envoy.

The introductory quatrains are an invocation to the poetic power and a tribute to those deciphering, calculating and classifying faculties which are its necessary supports. The principal themes and the characteristic paradoxes of the poem as a whole are here foreshadowed. Question changes by degrees into assertion; but at the same time spontaneous upsurge gives way to caution and delay. That hyperbole which is poetic utterance *par excellence* surges forth from the realm of memory, yet it is reliant, in order to become utterance at all, upon the representational procedures which are supplied by studious mental effort. Each of the mere procedures named with admirable succinctness in the eighth line is to be provided later in the poem with the things directly seen or felt which justify it and endow it with meaning: the atlas is given its magical island, the herbal its transcendent flowers and the ritual its supreme creative energy.

There is in the central section of the poem a residual imagery of travel and exotic escape. But although the ideal realm is presented as an island landscape – and a maritime or river setting is further suggested in quatrains 11 and 12 – no journey is recounted. The poet and his companion are simply in the landscape or not in it: there is no quest, no voyage to or fro. The sister is a complex presence. She may be thought of both as an independent person and as that which is most poet in the poet himself, whether this is conceived of as an intuitive power, an internal responsiveness (9.1–3) or as his highest gift for verbal expression (13.3–4). She is an aspect of his present personality and his remembered childhood self. (As we shall see, such shifts and fusions of identity are an important source of tension in the poem: we are likely to miss fine things if we underplay Mallarmé's statements of separateness and opposition between self and sister and assume in advance that the whole is a monodrama of the poet's self-awareness.) Although the poet's perception of the ideal realm is held to be instantaneous and unprepared, it is enacted in the poem as a deliberate process, moving by stages from an uncertain onset (3) to its moment of ecstatic culmination (8). The Idea-flowers[27] are introduced obliquely (5.1), in an appositional phrase and as an apparently accidental feature of the region in which they occur. Such defini-tion of the flowers as is provided in quatrains 4 and 5 is of a negative sort: the poet is here concerned with what these flowers are not (natural organisms) rather than with what they are, and with the effect they have on the least receptive part of himself, or of opinion at large. The syntax may be construed most productively on the plan: 'L'ère d'autorité se trouble / Lorsque...on dit / De ce midi... / Que...son site... / Ne porte pas de nom que cite / L'or de la trompette d'Été,' with 'Ils savent s'il a bien été' as a self-contained interpolation.

Even when Mallarmé moves on to his positive account of the flowers, and allows them their full clarity and self-sufficiency, an important uncertainty remains. Where have the flowers come from? The comparison referred to in the third quatrain ('O sœur, y comparant les tiens') would seem, until we read further, to set certain inward qualities of mind or soul beside the delights offered by the outward, sensible world. And this same world would appear to be again in question in the 'ce midi' of the fourth quatrain. But 'ce midi' – together with its extensions 'sol des cent iris' and 'site' – is itself involved in another, and quite different, comparison: it stands as the realm of *ideal* plants over and against all that is organically growing and botanically nameable. Therefore if we read the demonstra-tive adjective in 'ce midi' as a reference back to the 'paysage' of the previous quatrain, we must make a retrospective change in our reading of that quatrain: the charms compared will now be those of the mind on the one hand and of *ideality* on the other. (There is, of course, no necessity to read 'ce midi' like this: the phrase could refer to a region not previously named in the

poem; the change from past to present tense would support
this view.) An ambiguity of the same kind is present in '. . .
lacune / Qui des jardins la sépara' (7.3–4): does this mean that
the flowers are separate in kind from the palpable, growing
things to be found in terrestrial gardens? or that they stand out
with special clarity from the ideal gardens in which they occur?
The question is an important one. For it seems to me clear that
although no doubt is expressed in quatrains 3–8 about the
presence and the luminous power of the Ideas, the same lines
allow us to understand the relationship between the Ideas and
their human percipient in two different and scarcely compatible
ways. It all depends on the bridge the reader builds between 3
and 4. If he reads these quatrains as a continuous evocation of
one realm, he is likely to choose for '. . .lacune / Qui des jardins
la sépara' an interpretation akin to the second suggested above:
the poet and his companion will be in the ideal landscape at the
beginning of the narrative and remain there until a renewed
call to studiousness is heard at the end of 8. By the same token,
if he sees essential discrepancy rather than continuity at the
earlier stage, he is likely to catch an allusion to the same discrepancy later on: the poet and his companion will be despatched
abruptly from the world of sense into the world of Idea and
they will remain conscious in beholding the radiant Idea-
flowers of the lesser radiance they have left behind them. In the
one view the ideal is complete, self-subsistent and defiantly in-
different to the accidents of sense; the human subject has access
to it only when sensory appearances are found to have lost
their weight and dignity, or when they are wilfully put aside.
In the other view the ideal is discovered within the world of
sense; it has the more localised and more tenuous authority of a
mental construction put upon the changing diversity of things:
the human mind is drawn back and forth between the two
worlds, now seeking comfort among the ideal forms, now seeking to renew its energy among the hazards of sensory awareness. I shall return to this problem later.[28]

The poet is reminded at the moment of his highest contem-
plative fervour (8.4) that his own responsibilities as creator

remain to be fulfilled. By an exquisite transition he returns to the slow and patient execution of his task. Whereas poet and sister had before been united in their perception of the Idea-flowers, they re-appear from 9.1 as distinct personalities; the one seeks to recapture by mental effort the exaltation the other continues to feel. Quatrains 10–12 are the most difficult in the poem. The poet addresses the 'litigious' tendency of mind which would doubt that the events reported in the preceding narrative had occurred and which would expect evidence to be produced, and a case to be argued, even in the matter of self-transcendence. If he has nothing to say in support of his claim this does not mean that the Ideas do not exist but merely that they exceed the human power of comprehension ('...sache.../ Que de lis multiples la tige / Grandissait trop pour nos raisons, / Et non.../ Que ce pays n'exista pas.') The long subordinate clause which occupies most of 11 and 12 ('...comme pleure la rive /...s'écarte') is a set of jigsaw pieces from which several patterns of meaning may be formed. It is not easy to decide which of these patterns continues the argument of the poem most pertinently. However a reading which proceeded along the following lines would seem to me appropriate and to require but a small departure from grammatical convention. 'La rive' may be read as an elegant alternative for 'les riverains' – those who have stayed on the shore during the poet's island adventure. These shore-dwellers, who again typify the poet's sceptical hearers, lament that the island does not exist, and deny that the sense of elevation and amplitude reported by the poet had any proper basis. The poet is astonished to find that the failure of astronomy or geography to provide evidence of the ideal realm should be thought by his opponents sufficient grounds for claiming that no such realm exists.

At the end of the poem, as at the beginning, Mallarmé envisages the poetic impulse as finding its perfect outcome in the magical, creative activity of words. But what was then framed as a question has now become triumphant answer. The 'hyperbole' with which the poem began, and which is the model of poetic utterance, has now gathered substance and re-emerges in the proper names Anastase and Pulchérie. These names, the first from ἀνάστασις ('standing up', 'resurrection') and the second the French form of *Pulcheria* (and a whimsical Gallic feminine for *pulcher*), may be thought of as specimens of the supreme poetic language towards which the poet had previously aspired; they suggest a world of ritual performance in which the poet will at last, by his mastery of magical invocation, become adequate to the Ideas. By returning to the verbal dimension from the wordlessness of ecstasy, the poet is able to make his own tangible response to the inevitability of death. In dying he will leave his poem behind him as an enduring product of his own creative power. But the matter is urgent. For death threatens. And in any case the grave will eventually bear the poem as the poet's mocking epitaph. The last line of the poem is problematic in at least two ways: will name, or grave (or both) be hidden by the flower? does 'caché' mean 'veiled, obscured' or 'overshadowed in importance'? The most plausible reading appears to be that the still incomprehensible ideal flower is more powerful than the work by which the poet defies death, and more powerful too than death itself. Even as the poet faces the grave the flower remains as his spiritual protector and guarantor.

Looked at in one way, the movement of the poem is circular. Having summoned the power of words at the beginning, the poet goes on to recount his discovery of a realm beyond words. Having been fortified by this discovery, he returns at the end of the poem to his verbal task and prepares to meet the highest challenge to his creative capacities. But it is because this much has been brought so exactly to its point of completion and closure that Mallarmé is able to end without appearing indecisive upon a double metaphysical uncertainty. The nature of the Ideas and the nature of death remain as the mysteries which no words are equipped to solve, as permanent limits to the poet's power.

IV

Mallarmé is often thought to embody to perfection the disdainful rebellion of the artist against mass society, against a world that A. C. Bradley caricatured as one of 'trousers, machinery and policemen'.[29] What is more, a significant body of opinion still holds that Mallarmé made his poems as difficult as they are simply in order to prevent their assimilation by the vulgar. This notion is wrong, although not obviously and flatly so. For Mallarmé himself played an important part in putting the notion about and in encouraging certain of his admirers to see hermeticism as no more than an ingenious defensive weapon within the arsenal of 'sensibility'. In his early essay 'Hérésies artistiques: l'art pour tous' he complained that entry to the domain of poetry was scandalously easy, and called for a new poetic language which would lay down more stringent conditions for access:

> Ainsi les premiers venus entrent de plain-pied
> dans un chef-d'œuvre, et depuis qu'il y a des poëtes,
> il n'a pas été inventé, pour l'écartement de ces
> importuns, une langue immaculée, – des formules
> hiératiques dont l'étude aride aveugle le profane et
> aiguillonne le patient fatal; – et ces intrus tiennent
> en façon de carte d'entrée une page de l'alphabet où
> ils ont appris à lire!
> O fermoirs d'or des vieux missels! ô hiéroglyphes
> inviolés des rouleaux de papyrus!
> Qu'advient-il de cette absence de mystère?[30]

The essay ended on this exhortation to pride in caste:

> Que les masses lisent la morale, mais de grâce ne
> leur donnez pas notre poésie à gâter.
> O poëtes, vous avez toujours été orgueilleux;
> soyez plus, devenez dédaigneux.[31]

What has often escaped the notice of commentators, however, is that the essay gives no account whatever of the ways in which poetic texts are generated by their authors, or re-generated in the act of reading. Mallarmé is concerned to urge a personal attitude – one of respect for hard-won imaginative fulfilments – upon his reader and not to describe the internal characteristics of any real or hypothetical works of art. The essay does not entitle us to assume that Mallarmé in writing his poems took relatively simple and accessible ideas and gave them a protective veneer of complication; nor that the reader's proper task is to follow this process in reverse. The desire to prevent the work of art from being manhandled by an (imaginary?) population of coarse and irresponsible readers of poetry may have been a continuing incidental motive in Mallarmé's production of difficult poems, although there is little evidence for this. But such a desire is not an *artistic* motive, and has no explanatory value in describing the sense and structure of those works. The artistic motive which necessarily accompanies it, if the poems are to be anything other than mystifications, is the search for richer and more comprehensive kinds of meaning.

Later in this chapter I shall show that 'Prose' is difficult because problem-stating and problem-solving on many levels at once are part of its very point and substance and because the intellectual and imaginative operations that it requires us to perform in the solving cannot be made smoothly compatible. But it would be foolish to understate those features of the poem that have seemed to give support to the esoteric-élitist view of Mallarmé's art. To many new readers the poem is, with the possible exception of odd lines here and there, incomprehensible. Even the practised and sympathetic reader may find that the poem when approached in an impatient or inattentive frame of mind makes an unmistakable impression of hocus-pocus.[32] We are in a world of unstable entities. The personality of the poet–narrator may be split or re-unified with unnerving suddenness. There is no foreground of people against a background of things: inanimate objects and abstractions are performers in their own right, and play as large a part as the human agents in the development of the narrative. Mallarmé's terminology is not derived from one dominant intellectual field: metaphysics, geometry, rhetoric, the law, liturgy, taxonomy, geography, optics, psychology and more disciplines besides all add momentary colour and implication to the argument as it proceeds. There is no stable and enduring context to tell the reader, for example, whether the poet is referring to a hyperbole or a hyperbola at the beginning of the work, to unconsciousness rather than ignorance in the 'inconscience' of 4.4, or to reasoning powers rather than causes or explanations in the 'raisons' of 10.4. In each case the relative probabilities have to be decided by an examination of other and sometimes far-flung portions of text. And there is more than semantic uncertainty to trouble the newcomer. For effects of sound are obviously to the fore, and although certain readers will at once be arrested by these effects, and prompted by them to investigate the sense of the words, others may suspect the poet's auditory imagination to have gained the upper hand and sense-making to have fallen victim to some obscure but all-powerful phonetic impulse. The poem may strike readers of the second kind as at once uncomfortably rigid in matters of sound and uncomfortably slack in matters of sense.[33]

The tone in which Mallarmé conducts his argument may seem as resistant to explanation as the argument itself. A few words devoted to the subject by Henri Mondor describe this tone precisely: 'Ce qu'il y a, à la fois, dans *Prose*, de gravité et d'ironie, de pompe presque liturgique et d'allusions gracieuses, d'art poétique et de jeux de mots, d'île lointaine et paradisiaque, d'idéalisme platonicien...'.[34] What is not clear, however, is the system of values which underlies such contrary attitudes and allows them to exist side by side without doing one another damage. 'Prose' bears some resemblance to the work of the English metaphysicals. Here is that 'alliance of levity and seriousness' which T. S. Eliot saw as characteristic of 'metaphysical' wit;[35] here is their strongly argumentative manner. But the resemblance goes no further. For the climate of the poem is not favourable to those sudden enlargements or contractions of vision which are so important in, say, Herbert or Marvell, and by which these poets move back and forth between the domestic and the cosmic, the local and the universal. Consider again the phrase '...lacune / Qui des jardins la sépara'. If it is read in one of the ways I suggested earlier (as contrasting ideal and earthly flowers), the awful remoteness of matter from spirit, of sense from idea, has been closed by the word 'lacune' to a mere interstice; a tragic division within the mind of man has been seen, with delightful irony, as no worthier of regard than a lost word or a typographical error. But another reading (the 'lacune' as one detail of the ideal garden) competes for our attention and, as soon as we accept it, all but a trace of metaphysical wit disappears from the phrase. My point is simply that in 'Prose' Mallarmé allows his phrases in saying one thing to suggest a different or opposite thing, and that he gives a correspondingly small part to larger, more decisive changes of focus. However sensitive the reader may become to the changing tone of the poem he cannot be sure of what, exactly, it is in a given situation that disposes the poet to be grave or lighthearted. The personal or shared values which govern the fluctuations of tone in a metaphysical poem are easily deducible from the text itself, if not actually declared in it. In Mallarmé's poem this is not so. It is not the case, as has sometimes been suggested, that the poet's values are solidly present but obscured by ornament, but rather that on several central issues they have not been decided, or are beset by their contraries.

Much of the crucial detail of 'Prose' is presented in a remarkably oblique way. As a general feature of Mallarmé's style such obliqueness is often misunderstood. It is, of course, the product of an intimate temperamental bias. But the periphrases which his admirers cherish and his detractors abhor do not spring, as both parties sometimes claim, from a delicate refusal to be obvious or plain-spoken. Indeed it could with more justice be argued that, far from regarding plain statements with suspicion or distaste, Mallarmé was exceptionally conscious of the responsibilities he incurred in making them. The periphrases which enclose the many such statements (and the occasional *sententiae*) that appear in his verse and prose spell out with extreme caution the limiting conditions without which a proposition cannot be useful as an instrument of knowledge. That which the poet knows fully is thought worthy of the reader's inspection only when accompanied on the page by the things half-known and the uneasy conjectures from which it has emerged. But in 'Prose', as in all his finest poems, indirectness has a more creative role than that of enforcing the need for intellectual hesitancy and scruple. There are few of those long-winded refinements by which, according to Pope in *Peri Bathous*, a bad poet might convert 'shut the door' into:

> The woodden Guardian of our Privacy
> Quick on its Axle turn.[36]

The point is worth pausing over. For some slight fatuity of this kind may at first appear to surround such phrases as 'Car j'installe, par la science, / L'hymne des cœurs spirituels', 'Nous promenions notre visage', '...cette sœur.../ Ne porta son regard plus loin / Que sourire...' or 'L'enfant abdique son extase'. In each instance the mental activity referred to is easily grasped. But the reader may feel that more or weightier words have been used than 'the facts' require. What is interesting, however, is that none of these phrases introduces a separate, complicating strain of fancy into the poetic texture. They are all akin to one another and together constitute an important dimension of the poet's awareness. The 'excessive' verbs used by Mallarmé – *installer, promener, porter, abdiquer* – endow a set of mental acts with an air of physical performance. And in all cases except the third, ceremonious – that is prescribed and repeatable – conduct is suggested. Little remains to indicate that the poem is the record of an isolated occasion, or a short-lived personal excitement; all trace of wilfulness and appetite has been removed from the operations of the self. Upheavals of intellect or spirit are seen as having their place in a pre-ordained harmony of things. By these repeated suggestions of formality, of ceremony, of civilised disinclination to promote the needs of self, the poem moves towards that world of ritual perform-ance which Mallarmé evokes in the opening and closing quatrains.

V

With a half-dozen exceptions, Mallarmé's words are ordinary in 'Prose pour des Esseintes': most of them are drawn from the copper-coinage of everyday monosyllables. But his syntax is such as to make even the most self-effacingly functional of these words rich and strange.[37] For the poem contains a wealth of superimposed and interwoven messages, and demands of the reader who would enjoy this complexity fully an extreme effort of concentration. To read the poem successfully one has to devote a good deal of energy to the secondary operation of protecting messages proper from the marginal speculations to which Mallarmé's text gives rise, of excluding an uncomfortable semantic surplus from the mental field. Let me explain rather more exactly what I mean. As the receivers of written or spoken language we are often unable to know the meaning or grammatical status of a word until subsequent words have been given. For the most part such suspensions of sense pass unnoticed in ordinary usage. But the density of Mallarmé's poem, by compelling us to attend minutely to each word, gives them an unaccustomed prominence. Thus in reading 'sol des cent iris' (5.1) we may at first assume that the phrase is in apposition to 'ce midi' in the normal, backward-looking way; we learn on proceeding, however, that it is an anticipation of 'son site'. The inversion in 1.4 allows us to glimpse an illusory 'iron book' before the last word tells us that the book is merely *clad* in iron; the line-ending of 4.3 introduces a sufficiently long pause into 'notre double / Inconscience...' for a shared *Doppelgänger* to enter briefly upon the scene; 'monotonement' (or even 'songe monotonement') may be heard murmuring beneath the surface of 11.2; and so forth.

One way of looking at these fragile and grammatically unauthorised suggestions would be as a set of mere false leads which, even where they add a curiously 'appropriate' tincture to the sentences in which they occur, must be set aside if the general argument of the poem is to be kept intact. Such a view would represent the poem – in the language of the communications theorist – as a 'noisy channel', with a clear line of demarcation drawn between information and those random disturbances which inhibit its efficient transmission. But this distinction scarcely works in practice. For we reach our understanding of the text gradually and may often find as we proceed that apparent noise reveals itself to be message after all. Many of these suggestions would seem in any case to have been deliberately planted by Mallarmé; even as we reject them on one level in order to keep the surface of the text relatively tidy, they remain subliminally active and form a rich pattern of muted echoes.

In the cases I have mentioned so far the effort needed to deal with these suspensions of sense is, of course, small. But elsewhere the suspension may be so prolonged, and the possible leads so numerous, as to cause alarm and disarray in the reader's mind. At first sight quatrains 4–5 and 10–12 may not seem to be sentences at all: in both instances the lines may appear as the *disjecta membra* of an utterance, as a set of fragments over which syntax has no effective organising power.

By way of example I shall reconstruct certain of the steps and side-steps by which the decipherment of 4–5 might proceed. '. . . on dit / De ce midi' promises a statement. But when is this statement made? We cannot know whether 'que' in 4.3 is a pronoun or a conjunction until the clause it introduces is shown to be complete by the further 'que' of 5.1. No object other than 'midi' having been produced for 'approfondit', we realise that the first 'que' was a pronoun and that the statement is still to come. But is the 'que' of 5.1 conjunction or pronoun? Does it introduce the statement or a further relative clause? A glance over the remainder of the quatrain allows us to exclude the second possibility; and we may then assume that the statement is at last made in 5.2, with 'sol des cent iris, son site' as a slightly bizarre vocative phrase. But no. For 'ne porte pas' requires a subject and the only felicitous candidate is 'son site'. By this sort of back-formation the long-awaited statement may be elicited: '. . . son site / . . . Ne porte pas de nom que cite / L'or de la trompette d'Été.' 'Ils savent s'il a bien été' can only be a self-contained, interpolated sentence.

Such are the main problems the reader faces on approaching these lines. But even when he has grasped the entire sentence pattern and is able to find his bearings quickly at each re-reading, he continues to derive from the delays and detours of Mallarmé's syntax an acute sense that many alternative or subsidiary arguments remain to be examined. The principal message which he learns by degrees to extract from such a sentence retains an air of speculation and experiment.

Both these sentences (4–5, 10–12) are polemical in tone. But in each case the enemies or critics to whom the poet addresses himself, and whose objections he records, appear as the representatives of his own inner dissent: the fragmentary, self-frustrating movement of the syntax suggests that each utterance is being opposed at its source, that the existence and supreme value of the ideal realm are being asserted against a background of clamorous internal debate. By a characteristic paradox these dissenting voices are stronger on the second occasion, that is *after* the vision of the ideal flowers and exactly when we might expect their radiant self-evidence to have removed the poet's last doubts. The sentence which occupies 10–12 has two main propositions, both dependent upon the 'sache' of 10.1:

> i) 'que... la tige / Grandissait trop pour nos raisons,'
> ii) 'Et non... / Que ce pays n'exista pas.'

The second of these is an extreme case of ambiguity produced by what Empson has called the 'depraved negative'.[38] For the second term of its double negative is so far removed from the first as to acquire an independent negative force. The positive force of the entire proposition is further diminished by the climactic placing and the clinching tone of the second negative component: 'Que ce pays n'exista pas' is placed at the end of a sentence, at the end of a quatrain, at the end of a major subdivision of the argument; it resolves a complex syntactic pattern; it represents a return to clear statement after the gropings and bifurcations of 11.1–12.3. Furthermore it is also possible to read the clause as motivated by the 'attestés' of 12.2: in this case it is a negative not only in spirit but in fact. With its components distributed in this way the second half of the sentence enacts the opposite of what it means: the fact that the ideal country exists is proclaimed in such a way as to give generous support to those who protest that it does not. The splendid last line of 'Toast funèbre' has a comparable double status:

Et l'avare silence et la massive nuit.[39]

Silence and night have themselves been consigned to the grave by the enduring triumph of Gautier's poetry. But the monumental weight and symmetry of the line in which this defeat is finally sealed suggest not the disappearance of silence and night but their continuing, incontrovertible presence. In both cases the combined movement of negative and positive strains within the verse is analogous, in its psychological effect, to that of two melodies in counterpoint converging upon, and finding their resolution in, a single sustained note.

Until now my general contention has been that the involuted syntax of 'Prose pour des Esseintes' provides us with a varying picture of the speculative state of mind and invites us in reading some of the poet's propositions to remain aware of the contradictory mental impulses among which all propositions are born.[40] But the tortuous paths and false directions of speculative thinking are not represented in the poem merely to substantiate certain minor truths about mental process: the poem cannot be divided into a surface layer of important, formed thoughts and an underlayer of scrappy, stunted and discarded ones.[41] The choices we make in reading the syntactically complex sections of the poem have a direct influence on everything else the poem contains, even its central and relatively fixed motifs. A small adjustment of syntax may be sufficient to change the intensity of an idea, or the pattern of connections between ideas. I have already mentioned that irregularities in the conventional order of words or phrases may produce a set of 'false' secondary images. But the grammar of the poem may affect our imaginative activity in other ways. Without grasping the syntax we cannot fit the various landscape elements named in the poem into a visually coherent scene. And imagery may be produced *ex nihilo* once a completely non-concrete line has been provided with an adequate syntactic function; when lines such as 'Ils savent s'il a bien été' or 'Quand son jeu monotone ment' have been incorporated into the overall sentence pattern their latent sensory content is released. Whenever a new syntactic function is found for them this content changes.[42]

If we look at the poem more generally it is plain that its element of self-contradiction may prompt the reader to a good deal of creative activity on his own behalf. Mallarmé, in making this fictional world, was by no means strict in his adherence to that law of 'compossibility' which, according to Leibniz,[43] the divine creator himself chose to observe: the poet is quite willing to allow incompatible or mutually exclusive states of affairs to exist at once and in one place. He does not present us with one world held to be real, surrounded by enticing or distressing other worlds held to be virtual. His poem defines a region which is, in a phrase of Proust's, 'une et pourtant alternative',[44] a region where equipotential worlds converge. Certain readers will react to this with a sense of intellectual outrage and seek to re-introduce a real 'real world' endowed with its familiar prestige. But even readers who do not feel impelled to do this may find themselves inventing additional fictions with which to withdraw from contradiction – imaginary scenarios or conceptual schemes within which, for example, an island can both exist and not exist, a flower can be without extension yet capable of growth, words can perfectly embody, yet at the same time nullify, the objects they name.

In short, the images of 'Prose pour des Esseintes' are not of the sort that may be removed from the grammatical framework of the poem and lead an independent life in the reader's mind. For grammar has an activating, vitalising power over them; it tells us not simply how to see images, but what images are there to see. Mallarmé's adjustable syntax, far from providing us with a general impression of the speculative state of mind, requires of us that we enter that state of mind ourselves and bring our own power of construction and invention to bear upon the work in progress.

Simple statements, as I have suggested, play an important part in the poem. Following upon, and resolving, a sequence of periphrases or a passage of complex syntax,[45] these statements may give us a sudden sense of the intuitive power by which Mallarmé can 'by indirections find directions out'. But my reader may gather from what I have said until now that simplicity in 'Prose' is enormously outweighed by the poet's jealously guarded ingenuities. Before I go on to examine the verse-elements of the poem (and to describe further complexities) I must correct this initial impression and suggest how it is that a poem as complex as this is readable at all.

It is easy to imagine, in discussing poems which have a strongly ratiocinative manner (I am thinking, for example, of Shakespeare's 'The Phœnix and the Turtle', Marvell's 'The Garden', Baudelaire's 'Le Voyage', Valéry's 'Ébauche d'un serpent'), that reasoned argument has been the poet's major organising device during composition. As the argument of these poems is their main challenge to our understanding it is tempting to believe that simply by 'solving' this argument we answer all the important questions about their structure. But another, more primitive, method of construction may be used at the same time: much of the poem may be built by instalments, by the aggregation of equivalent parts. In the central stanzas of 'The Phœnix and the Turtle' (lines 25–48), for example, the theme of 'two distincts, division none' is reformulated on a dozen occasions; but on each occasion the underlying pattern – twoness resolved to oneness – remains intact. In Valéry's poem the serpent's principal boast, that the changeless realm of the One is incomparably poorer than the multifarious, changing and diffusive life of consciousness, is subject to exquisite variation throughout. While in 'Prose pour des Esseintes', as I have suggested earlier, the recurrent pattern is one of contrast between perception and performance, ecstasy and effort, unmediated insight and deliberate mental calculation.[46] As the argument of each poem branches out and becomes more complex, we learn more about this basic imaginative paradigm. Its surroundings change; it takes on new functions in the developing scheme of the poem. But its essential structure remains the same. A falsehood does not, of course, become true, nor a truth truer, merely by being repeated. Yet among the bafflements and indecisions of awareness which each poem explores, this simple pattern of repetition has a persuasive psychological effect upon the reader: it re-asserts the value of simplicity; it suggests that some knowledge at least is secure and that further knowledge based upon it is a worthwhile goal. Moreover it holds out the hope that this knowledge too, once achieved, will be a supremely simple thing.

VI

Maurice Grammont wrote in *Le Vers français*: 'Quand il y a conflit entre le mètre et la syntaxe, c'est toujours le mètre qui l'emporte, et la phrase doit se plier à ses exigences. Tout vers, *sans aucune exception possible*, est suivi d'une pause plus ou moins longue'.[47] Few people will dispute his second precept, if only because poets and competent speakers of verse so often turn these pauses to good effect. But what determines the length of Grammont's 'longer or shorter pause'? Although enjambement is sometimes thought to entail a suppression of the pause, the separation between run-on lines may be more usefully regarded as the minimum conventional pause. In the speaking or silent reading of poetry this minimum pause may be lengthened for one or more of the following reasons: (i) because the line-ending coincides with the ending of a stanza, or other section of the work, (ii) because the line-ending coincides with a syntactic break, (iii) because the rhymes are prominent and require of the reader a good deal of 'vertical' scanning between rhyme-words, (iv) because an additional expressive or dramatic effect is sought.

Of the three reasons which correspond to objective features of poetic texts, the third, concerning rhyme, is much the most important in 'Prose pour des Esseintes'. In Mallarmé's octo-syllables his rich rhymes take up an exceptionally large proportion of the line and sometimes all but monopolise it. In order to absorb the information provided by these rhymes the reader pauses for an unusually long time at the line-ending and in so doing gives each line-unit an unusual independence. Noun phrases occupying an entire line

L'hymne des cœurs spirituels
L'or de la trompette d'Été
La famille des iridées

are arrested and for a moment become 'things in themselves'; propositions occupying an entire line

L'ère d'autorité se trouble
Toute fleur s'étalait plus large
L'enfant abdique son extase

are given a sudden absoluteness by being insulated from everything which conditions them and limits their range of application. But phrases which have no grammatical claim to independence may be framed by silence in the same way: by analogy with the legitimately self-contained lines, the reader may convert such hybrids as 'Te lever, aujourd'hui grimoire', 'Que sourire et, comme à l'entendre' or 'Sous aucun climat, son aïeul' into grammarless, senseless, but strangely resonant formulae. One is reminded of the dramatic force that impossible phrases such as 'Tuba mirum' and 'Rex tremendae' sometimes acquire in settings of the Requiem mass.

At several points the sense of the poem is enhanced by these unusually palpable discrepancies between metre and syntax. The word 'lacune' in 7.3, for instance, is isolated in two different ways from the rest of the sentence: from what goes before by a syntactic pause and from what comes after by a metrical pause. (This is the only line in which exactly this happens to a single word; in each of the comparable cases – 'Idées' (8.1), 'Anastase' (13.3), 'Pulchérie' (14.3) – the second pause is dictated by syntax as well as metre.) The position of this word gives the entire phrase a more intense poignancy: preceded by one sort of gap and followed by an entirely different sort of gap, the word 'lacune' as a physical event becomes its own meaning. It becomes a lacuna, an imperfect interlocking, between systems. The reader has been provided with a new, tactile image with which to understand the separateness of flower from garden. The line-ending springs to life in much the same way in the middle of the ninth quatrain:

> ...cette sœur sensée et tendre
> Ne porta son regard plus loin
> Que sourire...

The metrical pause between lines 2 and 3 marks a limit and this must be exceeded if the syntax is to be completed, and the sense of the lines revealed. But limitation is the subject matter of these lines. Therefore while a boundary of one kind is being affirmed (the sister will not, or cannot, do more than she does) a boundary of another kind is being affirmed *and transgressed*. The pause demanded by metre suggests a momentary hesitation in the sister. Could the restriction placed upon the knowledge she bestows be waived as lightly as the poet's metrical restriction has been? But the truth and the poignancy of these incomparable lines lie in the way Mallarmé presents tenderness between people as an acknowledgement of difference, as a recognition that even where the desire to bestow and the desire to receive knowledge are perfectly attuned an obstinate barrier may remain. Could the restriction placed upon the sister's knowledge be necessary and irremovable? The line-ending gives its touch of physical immediacy to both kinds of question. *Heterogenea comparari non possunt* ... but there is one rule for the logician and for the poet quite another. Much of what is customarily called the 'suggestiveness' of poetry is the product of a wilful confusion of logical kinds. In instances like those I have mentioned operations which are logically incommensurate, but which have a common dynamic pattern, take place in extraordinarily close proximity; and we are not only encouraged to make a 'category mistake', an illicit comparison between metrical and semantic events, but positively rewarded for doing so.

In many more instances, however, the isolation of syntactically incomplete lines provides no such direct enhancement of sense. This would be all very well if the argument of the poem were not complex. Irrational single lines are often separated in the same emphatic way in comic verse or doggerel. But Mallarmé's stratified argument makes the reader attend closely to the forward movement of the text; it leads him to expect that later lines will complete the many patterns that earlier lines have foreshadowed. And while pursuing the overall sense within an utterance he may find that certain of its parts break loose from the syntax and enter into new relationships among themselves. Phrases which should be sequential and interdependent in order to meet the demands of syntax are made adjacent and equivalent by Mallarmé's heavily reinforced pauses. The effect is particularly noticeable in quatrains 1, 4, 7, 11, 12 and 14. We do not, of course, expect poets to allow metrical and semantic units to coincide for more than short stretches of verse; such matching soon produces an effect of monotonous redundancy. But in 'Prose' the two methods of organisation are not merely unsynchronised but placed in a competitive relationship; at one moment syntax will appear to be interfering with metre-felt-as-basic and at another, metre with syntax-felt-as-basic.[48] This is not the same thing as a conflict between rhythm and sense: it is a conflict between two kinds of sense, two 'sense-rhythms' one might almost say. For some sequences of lines may be read not only as argument but as a pattern of juxtaposed fragments. The affinities and contrasts to be observed between these fragments are in themselves a potent source of meaning.

The effects of this conflict should not be over-dramatised. Whatever disruptions occur within sentences, each sentence is finally reconciled with metre: each is completed by a full line at the end of a quatrain. And the rhyming elements which individualise each line – and create the problem – often serve in their joint action to clarify and heighten the developing argument. But the many moments of disharmony between metre and syntax do create a special sort of tension and a special sort of mystery.

Let me explain briefly why I use the word 'mystery' in this guarded fashion. A cursory examination of 'Prose pour des Esseintes' may lead one to the conclusion that the poem is in all important respects inscrutable, that Mallarmé's finest effects are simply inaccessible to analysis. Although this view is in some ways attractive (it relieves us, for one thing, of the obligation to think hard or straight), in its extreme form it can only impoverish the text. For if Mystery is seen as the poet's ultimate purpose and destination, it may seem singularly improper and fruitless for the reader to pursue clarity at all. In surrendering too hastily to the unknowable he may overlook those elements of the poem that are thoroughly systematic in character. The interactions of metre and syntax may indeed allow us a sudden glimpse into an unknown realm, a sudden sense that 'something far more deeply interfused' exists within the poem and within ourselves. But more often than not this sense of the unknown comes about because two independent sorts of *known* are being presented to us simultaneously. Each line of the poem has two kinds of identity and allegiance. At any moment a perspective may change and the words we are reading may be transferred from one pattern to another. The one set of words supports two kinds of vision and of intellectual coherence. We are not in a shadowy world of suggestions and half-meanings, but in a middle zone where clear and whole meanings intersect. I shall return to this matter later and discuss in more detail Mallarmé's delight in twoness and the joint life of systems.[49]

VII

The phonetic properties of words, like the metrical system itself, figure prominently in the foreground of 'Prose pour des Esseintes'. In both matters the reader is asked to set aside certain of the expectations with which he usually approaches 'serious' poetry, and which he finds so comfortably confirmed in the work of Mallarmé's immediate predecessors. The poet has created a new – and some may think scandalous – balance between the semantic function of words and the life they lead as physical things. The meaning(s) and the grammatical role of an individual word have often to be worked out by an elaborate process of deduction and cross-checking within the text. But long before these calculations are complete the word has assumed its place in an intricate system of physical parities and disparities. And the direction in which our calculation of meaning proceeds may be suggested or endorsed by the pressure of the sound and rhythm systems. As we gain experience of the poem, the relationship between sound and meaning becomes more properly reciprocal. They grow together to form a remarkably close tissue: at each re-reading sounds may suggest new meanings and meanings newly grasped may prompt us to an awareness of further phonetic likenesses. In this poem Mallarmé's end-rhymes are richer – both as sonorities and as sources of information – than those to be found in any nineteenth-century French poem of comparable intensity or involvement. Other sorts of phonetic correspondence between words – assonance, alliteration, internal rhyme and homonymy – also occur often. But the habits of perception which we develop in response to the extraordinary end-rhymes give these other affinities of sound an even larger importance than their number would lead us to anticipate. The texture of Mallarmé's verse provides so many fruitful sound–meaning connections that it will be impossible for most readers to hold them all in mind at once. On any one occasion most of these connections will be present not in articulate form, but as a background murmur: the reader will have a sense of countless small patterns being created, tenuously surviving, and disappearing just beyond the threshold of full conscious awareness.[50] But although every reading of the poem will of necessity leave much of the material untouched, no reading can claim to be complete without assigning a role to this underlying richness of implication.

Before I go on to examine these sound properties more closely I shall quote some passages from Roman Jakobson's brilliant and provocative essay on 'Linguistics and Poetics'.[51] Although Jakobson's remarks and definitions are extremely general in their scope, they will be seen to have a peculiar relevance to the texture of Mallarmé's later verse. In the first passage Jakobson is seeking to determine 'the empirical linguistic criterion of the poetic function'. He asks '...what is the indispensable feature inherent in any piece of poetry?' 'To answer this question', he continues

> we must recall the two basic modes of arrangement used in verbal behavior, *selection* and *combination*. If 'child' is the topic of the message, the speaker

selects one among the extant, more or less similar,
nouns like child, kid, youngster, tot, all of them
equivalent in a certain respect, and then, to comment
on this topic, he may select one of the semantically
cognate verbs – sleeps, dozes, nods, naps. Both
chosen words combine in the speech chain. The
selection is produced on the base of equivalence,
similarity and dissimilarity, synonymity and
antonymity, while the combination, the build up
of the sequence, is based on contiguity. *The poetic
function projects the principle of equivalence from the axis
of selection into the axis of combination.* Equivalence is
promoted to the constitutive device of the
sequence.[52]

He quotes a passage from Hopkins on the importance of
parallelism in poetry and translates it as follows into his own
terminology: '...equivalence in sound, projected into the
sequence as its constitutive principle, inevitably involves semantic equivalence, and on any linguistic level any constituent of
such a sequence prompts one of the two correlative experiences
which Hopkins neatly defines as "comparison for likeness'
sake" and "comparison for unlikeness' sake"'.[53] The same point
is stated as a formula later in the essay: 'In poetry, any conspicuous similarity in sound is evaluated in respect to similarity
and/or dissimilarity in meaning'. For Jakobson this super-
imposition of similarity on contiguity 'imparts to poetry its
throughgoing symbolic, mutiplex, polysemantic essence...'.[54]
Jakobson's essay is intended not as a guide to the detection of
successful poems, but as a description of one especially important way in which sense in poems is produced. What his theory
in no way disallows – how could it? – is that conspicuous or
elaborate equivalences may prove to have a low or an irrelevant
semantic yield. Trivial sound-patterning exists; Hopkins, for
all his lucidity as a prosodist, was himself capable of it.

In 'Prose' Mallarmé is – to put the matter in its simplest
terms – more 'throughgoing' than most poets in his use of

internal parallelism and equivalence. I have already mentioned, in my remarks on metre and syntax, one important way in which similarity is superimposed upon contiguity. Further examples will occupy several of the pages which follow. These features are worth examining at some length not because the poem is an exceptionally dense pattern of criss-crossing parallelisms, but because these parallellisms create or intensify meaning in an exceptionally vigorous way. The poem contains, it cannot be denied, a welter, a Byzantine superabundance, of information: interesting new facets of the thing rise in fearful profusion to meet the analytic gaze. But the poem is so toughly and coherently conceived as a piece of thinking that little of this information is properly redundant: the argument is broad enough to accommodate a wealth of incidental suggestions and subtle enough to produce a creative interplay between them.

VIII

Certain of the ways in which Mallarmé exploits assonance and alliteration[55] are entirely traditional, in that the phonetic relationship between parts of two or more words reinforces another relationship between those words. For example,
a person/object may be bound closer to her/its attribute:

> *s*œur *s*en*s*ée
> *li*s mu*l*tip*l*es
> *g*rand *g*laïeul

two attributes to each other:

> se*n*sée et te*n*dre

two ideas (in apposition) to each other:

> *lu*cide *c*ontour, *l*acu*ne
> [Gloire du long] *dé*sir, I*dé*es,

an agent to its action:

> *t*ou*t*e f*l*eur s'é*t*a*l*ait
> La fam*i*lle des *i*ridées/Su*rg*ir

an action to a mode of action:

Triompha*l*ement ne sais-tu/*Te le*ver

Certain phrases are packed with corresponding sounds: 'cette sœur sensée et tendre' contains the vowel pattern [ãeeã] and the consonant pattern [stsʀsstʀ]; 'de lis multiples la tige' has [əiiəi] and [lltllt]; 'Gloire du long désir, Idées' has [eiie] and [lʀdldʀd]. In each of these instances assonance and alliteration give an additional tightness and cogency to the phrase: phonetic similarities within the phrase make it more persuasive and more memorable.[56]

The examples I have given so far are at a medium level of prominence. But some of Mallarmé's assonances and alliterations are less and some considerably more prominent than this. Criticism is now well equipped to detect these verse features in their subtler and less explicit forms. I shall mention three useful lines of approach and show briefly how each is applicable to 'Prose pour des Esseintes'. Grammont noted that the poet may emphasise a word by repeating not the word itself but its 'essential and characteristic phonemes'.[57] He gives this couplet from Hugo's 'La Conscience' as an example:

Il réveilla *s*es fil*s* dormant, *s*a femme la*ss*e,
Et *s*e rem*i*t à fu*i*r *sinistre* dans l'e*s*pace.[58]

In an article on 'Phonological Aspects of Style', Dell H. Hymes has examined the same process as it takes place within whole poems.[59] He has isolated what he calls 'summative' words within certain English sonnets. (For a word to have summative force it must contain sounds prominent in the poem, express the theme of the poem and be placed so as to have a culminating effect.[60]) Kenneth Burke has argued that phonetic cognates ([bpm] or [tdn], for example), appearing in concealed alliterations, are an important and neglected source of musicality in verse.[61]

'Prose pour des Esseintes' is particularly well endowed with such patterns of sound. The effect observed by Grammont is to be found in several instances:

Ne *porte* pas de n*om* que ci*te*
L'*or* de la *trompette* d'Été.

(5.3-4)

*Q*ue sou*ri*re et, *c*omme à l'*ente*ndre
J'o*cc*upe mon *antique* soin.

(9.3-4)

D'ouïr *t*out le *C*iel et *l*a *ca*r*te*
*S*ans fin *attestés s*ur mes p*as*,

(12.1-2)

The searcher for summative words will find in 'Pulchérie' a perfect example: it represents the culmination of Mallarmé's argument; together with 'Anastase', its equivalent in grammatical case, syntactic and metrical position, and number of syllables, it answers and modifies the opening exclamation of the poem; 'Pulchérie' and 'Hyperbole' have four phonemes in common [plʀi] and of these the consonants have appeared, in sequence or with one other consonant intervening, on 14 further occasions. A total of 16 appearances within 56 octosyllabic lines would appear to be unusually high,[62] although what matters is not so much the number of repeated sounds as the power of the text as a whole to provide those sounds with semantic motivation. The concealed patterns noted by Burke are to be found in many places. Lines 5.3–6.2 contain an extraordinary mesh of dental consonants: [ntdnt]; [dtdt]; [dn]; [dnd]. And quatrain 11 has a similar wealth of nasal consonants and vowels: [nɔ̃m]; [ɑ̃ɔ̃mnnmɑ̃]; [ɑ̃]; [mmɔ̃nnmɑ̃].

No point would be served by completing this catalogue. For the effect of these delayed or disguised equivalences of sound remains, in any intelligent reading of the poem, largely subliminal. They have no designs upon us: they are not imitative; they do not form 'sound symbolisms' or cryptograms. The important thing about them is exactly that they are parities, samenesses, that the poem as it probes and explores is being provided with an additional set of ligatures. Even as Mallarmé's thought investigates difference, this 'air ou chant sous le texte', as he called it,[63] minutely but firmly reminds us of similarity.

Repeated sounds may also be much more conspicuous than is necessary for the reinforcement of sense that I began by describing. Up to a certain frequency, alliteration and assonance tend to encourage credence by increasing the internal solidity of the phrase, but beyond that point we may suspect trickery or facetiousness on the poet's part. It is a matter of retaining a balance between diversity and uniformity: sounds repeated often and with short intervals between each appearance will suggest nagging insistence; they will draw attention to themselves as mere sound:

> Que, *s*ol des *c*ent *iris*, *s*on *s*ite,
> *Ils s*avent *s'il* a bien été,[64]

$$(5.1-2)$$

Here the recurrent phonemes in no way imitate physical action, as do Racine's in:

> Pour qui sont ces serpents qui sifflent sur vos têtes ?[65]

or Valéry's in:

> Vous me le murmurez, ramures!...Ô rumeur[66]

In the first of Mallarmé's lines the repeated consonant and the repeated vowel are all the more likely to strike the reader as an unmotivated display of sound because the connections which they supply are superinduced upon phrases which are already strongly connected by apposition and in no need of further emphasis. And when, as in this and many smaller instances, the poet oversteps a metrical and a syntactic boundary in his pursuit of sound likeness, repetition may appear to undermine rather than fortify his utterance. Sense may be driven awry by processions of like sounds, or by sounds which establish unreasonable and intrusive links between remote parts of a sentence. I do not consider the last lines I quoted from the poem to be defective, although I imagine that few people will find them gratifying to the ear. Their insistent sounds have an important contribution to make to the discontinuous sentence in which they occur, and they make it precisely by cutting across the main drift of Mallarmé's meaning. They create a sudden powerful sense of unity regained, of difference resolved, but long before any such sense has been earned in argument: the struggle between doubt and certainty which Mallarmé portrays in these quatrains is given a further element of anxiety by prematurely reaching, and ineffectually passing, its point of decision.

Mallarmé's assonance and alliteration do not provide the poem with a sustained and euphonious flow of sound.[67] Their general effect is quite different from the continuous modulation, the splendid phonetic interlacing, which often sustains Valéry's verse for long paragraphs. Where Mallarmé's repeated phonemes are prominent they are crowded together in batches, and between the batches there is seldom a smooth transition: we are moved abruptly from one dominant sound pattern to another, often phonetically remote from it. (The effect resembles that of contrasted blocks of instrumental colour as used in orchestral music.) For the most part the concealed patterns too operate on a small scale. The recurrent [plʀ] figure I mentioned earlier no doubt creates some impression of overall phonetic continuity. The ghostly 'fore-rhymes' which are often to be heard between the beginnings of successive lines may also be thought to have this tendency. Such echoes between line-openings – which will vary in prominence according to the semantic and metrical stress which the words concerned bear – are produced by rhyme proper:

> Et *non* comme pleure la rive
> Quand *son* jeu monotone ment　　　　　　(11.1–2)

> Avant *qu'un* sépulcre ne rie
> Sous au*cun* climat, son aïeul,　　　　　　(14.1–2)

by an ablaut (changing vowels within a fixed frame of consonants):

> *Sur* maints charmes de paysage,
> O *sœur*, y comparant les tiens.　　　　　　(3.3–4)

L'ère d'autorité se trouble
*Lors*que, sans nul motif, on dit   (4.1–2)

Que, *sol* des cent iris, son site,
Ils savent *s'il* a bien été,   (5.1–2)

De *por*ter ce nom: Pulchérie!
Caché *par* le trop grand glaïeul.   (14.3–4)

by the contraction of a relatively complex phonemic pattern to
a relatively simple one:

De *ce* m*idi* que notre double [sii]
Incon*sci*ence approfondit   [sj]   (4.3–4)

Que *de* l*is* multiples la tige
Gran*diss*ait trop pour nos raisons,   (10.3–4)

or by a general re-shuffling of like sounds:

N*e por*te p*as* de nom que cite
L'*or* de l*a t*rompette d'Été.   (5.3–4)

Oui, *d*ans *un*e île que l'air charge
De v*ue* et *n*on de visions   (6.1–2)

D'un luc*ide* contour, lacune   [dœ̃id]
Qu*i d*es jar*dins* la sépara.   [iddɛ̃]   (7.3–4)

But the antiphonal play which takes place between fore-rhyme
and end-rhyme contributes more to the internal economy of
the quatrain than to the onward flow of the whole poem. This
double pivotal movement, in which endings are counter-
balanced by beginnings and alternate by successive pairs of
lines, helps to protect the end-rhymes from the thudding four-
squareness to which these exceptionally rich sonorities are
prone; and it makes the quatrain into a cohesive sound-unit.
In a single instance only are two quatrains joined by such
echoes. This case is a remarkably suggestive one, and not least
because it reproduces an earlier (3.3–4) rhyme of this kind:

*Sur*gir à *ce* nouveau devoir,

Mais *c*ette *sœur* sensée et tendre   (8.4–9.1)

In short, rather than suggest by continuously interwoven assonances and alliterations that his poem represents a single unbroken span of awareness, Mallarmé often uses these devices to individualise the syntactic and metrical elements of which the poem is composed and to dramatise its internal differences.

IX

Until now I have been describing mainly the casual, short-term symmetries which Mallarmé introduces into the text by matching single phonemes. Before I discuss the altogether more systematic activity which is rhyming, I should clarify an important general point about these many effects of sound. It will have become clear that the poet in practising his ingenious linguistic economies, in turning his phonetic materials to new and often improbable uses, gives his poem an atmosphere of self-consciousness and contrivance. Sounds that have gone before appear to possess an unusually high capacity to determine those that are to come. What is more, the poem by its close network of repeated sound figures creates the delightful illusion that it is a self-generating verbal universe. And it becomes a rough and ready working model of the innovation process that operates within the language as a whole. In his *Cours de linguistique générale*, Saussure observed, taking a characteristic pleasure in much from little: 'La langue est une robe couverte de rapiéçages faits avec sa propre étoffe [. . .] L'immense majorité des mots sont, d'une manière ou d'une autre, des combinaisons nouvelles d'éléments phoniques arrachés à des formes plus anciennes.'[68] In the same way, 'Prose pour des Esseintes' is made by the constant and often conspicuous re-combination of elements from its own past. Mallarmé has written a wittily compressed – and to the unwary a most misleading – history of the language. To increase the self-awareness of the language is, of course, among the traditional tasks of the poet.[69] Mallarmé is unusual, in this as in so many other aspects of the poem, not for what he does but for the suggestiveness and concentration of his performance.

For the moment I shall illustrate this by reference to a single 'fact of language' as it appears in quatrains 4–6. These contain a profusion of homophones quite without parallel in the remainder of the poem:

> *L'ère* d'autorité *se* trouble
> Lorsque, *sans* nul motif, on dit
> De *ce* midi que notre double
> Inconscience approfondit
>
> Que, sol des *cent* iris, son *site*,
> *Ils* savent s'*il* a bien *été*,
> Ne porte pas de *nom* que *cite*
> L'or de la trompette d'*Été*.
>
> Oui, dans une *île* que *l'air* charge
> De vue et *non* de visions
> Toute fleur s'étalait plus large
> *Sans* que nous en devisions.

Homophony is not usually regarded as a fertile source of poetic effect. And rightly. Stephen Ullmann concludes his valuable account of homonymy in general as follows:

> ...la valeur stylistique des équivoques homony-
> miques est très inférieure à celle de l'ambiguïté
> polysémique. Leurs effets manquent de subtilité.
> Le suspens qu'elles produisent est momentané, et
> le jeu une fois saisi, il n'en reste rien qu'un amuse-
> ment quelque peu dédaigneux. L'écart entre les
> sens, leur disparité foncière qui est le trait distinctif
> de l'homonymie, explique qu'il n'en sort, en
> général, que de mauvais jeux de mots et des
> artifices futiles.[70]

The conventional way of using homophones had been to com-press the drama of sound-likeness and sense-unlikeness into a single instant by placing the homophonous pairs together, as in these lines by Jean Molinet:

Molinet n'est sans bruit ne sans *nom, non*;
Il a *son son* et comme tu *vois, voix,*
Son doulx *plait plait* mieux que ne fait *ton ton*;
Ton vif *art art* plus cler que char*bon bon*;[71]

In Mallarmé's quatrains the pairs are in direct contact in both rhymes of 5 (and this is sufficiently unusual as an event – the only other such rhyme in the poem being the *pas*: *pas* of 12 – to alert us to the presence of further correspondences).[72] But for the rest his verbal wit is exquisitely subdued; the identical sounds, reappearing irregularly and often at long intervals, add a mere undercurrent of suggestion to the texture of the verse.

Quatrain 6 contains four homonymic references back to the preceding quatrains (*île*:*il*/*ils*; *l'air*:*l'ère*; *non*:*nom*; *sans*:*cent*); minute connecting threads are thereby cast between two of the most obviously separate sections of the poem, between 4–5 which are anxious disputation about the existence of the island-flowers and 6–8 which affirm their simple self-evidence. We are not being openly invited, as we are by rhyme, to scan the word-pairs for semantic kinship – which does not mean, of course, that interesting links are not to be found: names and negations, a hundred and 'withoutness', may be thought of as versions of the more general polarity between plenitude and emptiness which the poem sets forth; a plain metonymic connection exists between *ils* (iris), *il* (son site) and *île*; *l'air* brings to the surface an important connotation of *l'ère*: the worrying thing about the era referred to in 4.1 was exactly its *air d'autorité*. But although the reader can read well without working these relationships out, or perceiving them at all, the effect of Mallarmé's fourfold echo is not simply an acoustic one. For the poet in re-arranging particles of sound in which doubt had been enacted comes up with the very formula for certainty: doubt words, far from being superseded, are converted as we read into certainty words. In the slender exchanges which thus take place between these quatrains, we may for a moment grasp the nature of Mallarmé's ideal tacit poetry, his 'poëme tu, aux blancs'.[73] As I suggested earlier, new meanings produced so economically within a restricted sound-compass bring our attention to bear upon the poem as linguistic process: even as the island looms up in its self-evident 'thereness' at the beginning of 6, we are encouraged to feel that it is not only the subject but the product of poetic discourse. In its context of intense verbal play, the emphatic *Oui* which introduces the quatrain expresses not only a metaphysical conviction about the Ideal realm, but a practical trust in the generative power of the word.

The question will often arise for the analyst of texts who notices these delicate threads: what exactly am I discovering? Are these subdued parities of sound the results of chance encounter or of conscious artistic choice? Did the artist *intend* all this? Here again the example of Saussure is instructive. His research into the Latin poets' use of anagrams[74] shows the same fascination with the economy and productivity of language that appears so often in his work on linguistics. Saussure was distressed by the sheer quantity of concealed anagrams that he brought to light and unable to decide whether he had hit upon an esoteric principle of composition that had survived unpublicised throughout a centuries-old tradition, or upon a mere chance effect of alphabetical permutation. Jean Starobinski, in his penetrating presentation of Saussure's notebooks, has written as follows on the dilemma; in these paragraphs, which are the wisest that I know on the subject, the commentator on Mallarmé can find comfort, and at the same time a just reminder of the limitations of his quest:

> Saussure s'est-il trompé? S'est-il laissé fasciner
> par un mirage? Les anagrammes ressemblent-ils
> (*sic*) à ces visages qu'on lit dans les taches d'encre?
> Mais peut-être la seule erreur de Saussure est-elle
> d'avoir si nettement posé l'alternative entre 'effet
> de hasard' et 'procédé conscient'. En l'occurrence,
> pourquoi ne pas congédier aussi bien le hasard que
> la conscience? Pourquoi ne verrait-on pas dans
> l'anagramme un aspect du *processus* de la parole, –
> processus ni purement fortuit ni pleinement

conscient ? Pourquoi n'existerait-il pas une itération, une palilalie génératrices, qui projetteraient et redoubleraient dans le discours les matériaux d'une première parole à la fois non prononcée et non tue ? Faute d'être une *règle* consciente, l'anagramme peut néanmoins être considérée comme une *régularité* (ou une loi) où l'arbitraire du mot-thème se confie à la nécessité d'un processus. L'erreur de Ferdinand de Saussure (si erreur il y a) aura aussi été une leçon exemplaire. Il nous aura appris combien il est difficile, pour le critique, d'éviter de prendre sa propre trouvaille pour la règle suivie par le poète. Le critique, ayant cru faire une découverte, se résigne mal à accepter que le poète n'ait pas consciemment ou inconsciemment *voulu* ce que l'analyse ne fait que *supposer*. Il se résigne mal à rester seul avec sa découverte. Il veut la faire partager au poète. Mais le poète, ayant dit tout ce qu'il avait à dire, reste étrangement muet. Toutes les hypothèses peuvent se succéder à son sujet : il n'acquiesce ni ne refuse.[75]

X

Mallarmé had the special gift that Banville, in his witty and impassioned treatise on verse, called 'l'imagination de la Rime'.[76] And 'Prose pour des Esseintes' has good claim to be considered as Mallarmé's boldest exploitation of this gift. But although the brilliance of his rhyming in 'Prose' has not gone unrecognised, it has often failed to win critical approval : it has been presented as an irresponsible flirtation with an archaic mode, as the thrusting of a faded ornamental style upon an otherwise austere and strong-minded argument.[77] Such misgivings are easy enough to explain. Mallarmé elaborately exploits two rhymes which have never had a wide range of uses : ultra-rich rhyme (the *rime léonine*) and punning rhyme (the *rime équivoque* or *équivoquée*).[78] Both have their place within popular rhyming tradition. And from the time of the *grands*

rhétoriqueurs both were favoured as instruments of verbal display
by the professional wit, the *précieux* and the courtly encomiast.
Rabelais uses the *rime équivoque* in parodying the manner of the
rhétoriqueurs; du Bellay flatly proscribes it, while recommending
rich rhyme in general as a source of musicality in verse.[79]
Precisely because these rhymes are at once unusually specialised
and unusually memorable, Mallarmé's reader may find the
poem laden with seemingly incongruous reminiscences. The
penultimate quatrain, for example:

> L'enfant abdique son extase
> Et docte déjà par chemins
> Elle dit le mot: Anastase!
> Né pour d'éternels parchemins,

shares one kind of verbal energy with these lines from an epistle
by Guillaume Cretin to his poetic master:

> Lettres allez sans sejourner en place,
> Que ne soyez es mains de Molinet;
> Et le gardez que desir mol il n'ayt
> A m'escripre, mais vouloir bien ample a ce.[80]

or with these from the door of the Abbey of Thélème:

> Voz abus meschans
> Rempliroient mes camps
> De meschanceté
> Et par faulseté
> Troubleroient mes chants
> Vos abus meschans[81]

While in such lines as these from the eleventh quatrain:

> Quand son jeu monotone ment
> . . .
> Parmi mon jeune étonnement

Mallarmé is close to those experiments in 'total rhyme' of which
the following ingenious inanity, usually attributed to Banville,
is a characteristic product:

Dans ces meubles laqués, rideaux et dais moroses,
Danse, aime, bleu laquais, ris d'oser des mots roses.[82]

Mallarmé's rhymes are one among several features of the poem which place it marginally but firmly within the traditions of elegant artifice and comic word-play. That Mallarmé's adherence to these traditions should be thought grounds for critical complaint betrays a restrictive and wholly misguided notion of poetic 'seriousness'.[83] The gaiety and learned wit of the poem, far from damaging the dignity of its philosophical themes, add considerably to their emotional complexity. Yet there is much more to the rhymes than this. They are central, as I shall show, to the imaginative and intellectual fabric of the poem. As so little has been written about the rhymes as they actually behave *in situ*, I shall begin by making one or two elementary mechanical observations.

Samuel Daniel, defending rhyme against Campion's charge that it offered mere 'childish titillation', claimed for it an important psychological function: rhymes provided the reader of verse with a known frame having 'those due staies for the minde, those incounters of touch as makes the motion certaine, though the varietie be infinite'.[84] In a poem as copiously argued as 'Prose' this rhythmic, stabilising function of rhyme is particularly important. So much about the poem, and especially Mallarmé's self-entangling argumentative manner, prevents us from forming useful 'mental sets', from maintaining an expectation of order as we read, that predictable sound-likeness provides us with a necessary guarantee that order remains possible. Rhymes, placed within this involved and often distracting texture, come to represent the principles of invariance and symmetry. They individualise the line as a metrical unit;[85] they encourage us to connect ideas analogically; and on the phonetic level they remove all trace of nervous fidgeting from the operations of assonance and alliteration: the partial, glancing collisions which take place within and between the lines are regularly resolved, at the line-ending, to full homophonic impact.

The 'vertical' rhythm which is created by rhyme, and

strengthened by the strictly regular alternation of masculine and feminine endings, is prevented from becoming grossly emphatic or metronomically rigid by all manner of variations in the size and structure of the rhyme-units. Although the reader quickly becomes aware that any given rhyme is much more likely than not to be rich (*rimes riches* outnumber *rimes suffisantes* by 25 to 3, and the latter all occur in the second half of the poem), he has no means of predicting the exact point in the line where the rhyming elements will begin. There is no overall tendency, for example, for rhyme to increase or decrease in richness as the poem proceeds, or for the first rhyming pair within a quatrain to be richer or less rich than the second. The *rimes équivoques* are unevenly spread; and the sudden harmonic change which they introduce during the central climax of the poem (6 and 7 have one pair each; 8 has two pairs) softens rather than strengthens our larger sense of periodicity.

Two of the ways in which variety is achieved are of special interest. First, assonance and alliteration may exist between phonemes which adjoin the rhyme-units proper: *où nous nous taisons:pour nos raisons* (10); *litige:la tige* (10); *sépulcre ne rie: Pulchérie* (14) (readers who choose the etymologically more appropriate pronunciation [pylkeʀi] will discover a further common sound); and so forth. Secondly, they may exist between successive rhymes within a quatrain: the rhymes of 5 have [t] throughout; those of 8 [d] and [ʀ]; those of 7 and 12 [a]; [j] alternates with [i] in those of 2, and [ɑ] with [a] in those of 13. Mallarmé allows assonance between successive rhymes[86] in the face of a powerful convention to the contrary. The effect is odd: we hear against the dovetailed phonetic contrasts of the rhymed quatrain a distant echo of the antique assonantal *laisse*.

What is noteworthy in both these cases is that a gratifying sense of diversity within rhyme can be created by the introduction of further uniformities.[87] How is it that assonance and alliteration can still have this effect in a work which is all but saturated in them? The answer is of course that these additional correspondences belong unmistakably to the rhyme axis; in creating further 'vertical' relationships between lines they do not interfere with the pattern of 'horizontal' relationships within lines. For these connecting routes are so clearly dominant in the production of meaning, and so firmly counterbalance each other, that the reader quickly develops the habit of simultaneous, two-way scansion. Thus in the tenth quatrain, for example, he may absorb the linear relationships:

> Oh! sache *l'*Esp*ri*t de *li*tige,
> A c*e*tte heure *où nou*s *nou*s ta*i*sons,
> Que de *li*s mu*l*ti*pl*es *l*a *ti*ge
> Grandiss*ai*t trop pour nos r*ai*sons,

without any sense that these are being contaminated by the interlinear relationships in which the same phonemes are involved: *li*tige:*l*a *ti*ge; *où nou*s *nou*s ta*i*sons:*pou*r *n*os r*ai*sons. At different moments within the unfolding of the poem a single phoneme thus has different identities, sharply distinguishable according to the axis in which it is placed. The strength of these two axes is such that most readers will fail to notice in normal reading the many diagonal relationships which a close inspection of the sound texture reveals. (In the above quatrain, for example, a direct parity is unlikely to be sensed between the sequence [dəli] at the end of the first line and the same sequence at the start of the third.) By means of this simple underlying geometry the poet is able to give assonance and alliteration an important subsidiary function in rhyme without smothering his argument in identical sounds. This is of course the standard geometry for a poem in octosyllables. For such lines are not divided by caesura into the equivalent segments between which diagonal cross-reference can readily take place. Mallarmé's achievement is to have given a completely new authority to the rhyme axis and to have found in the joint operation of the two axes a brilliantly economical way of organising and storing a complex abundance of information.

XI

Prosodists have traditionally been silent, or at best timid and non-committal, on rhyme as an instrument of meaning.[88]

Certain literary critics, on the other hand, regarding this as a non-technical matter falling naturally within the province of criticism, have exaggerated the power of rhyme: they have treated the rhyming words as the participants in a disembodied micro-drama, as a two-term shorthand which mysteriously epitomises the larger senses of a poem while remaining for practical purposes unconnected to that poem. Few have treated the question as sensibly as W. K. Wimsatt in his short and suggestive paper on 'One Relation of Rhyme to Reason'.[89] Wimsatt argued that 'verse in general, and more particularly rhyme, make their special contribution to poetic structure in virtue of a studiously and accurately semantic character'. And he insisted, as if in anticipation of the later 'separatist' view of rhyme to which I referred, that 'words have no character as rhymes until they become points in a syntactic succession'.[90]

In the next few pages I shall present a tentative semantic view of Mallarmé's rhymes in 'Prose pour des Esseintes'. I shall outline some of the ways in which rhyme enforces, modifies, inflects or contradicts the meanings of the poem. A special sort of pleasure is to be had from the systematic operations of rhyme. But my own view, which I shall state dogmatically and in advance of my analysis, is that rhyme is pleasurable in so far as its system is empowered to affect the primary materials, sensory and intellectual, of which the poem is made. Remove the rhymes from this or any other poem, schematise them, introduce all manner of subsidiary control mechanisms into your scheme and you are left with system, but system of the dullest and dimmest. No feature of poetry, be it never so finely or so variously analysed, can compete with, say, logic or mathematics in the supply of self-supporting intellectual structure. Yet rhyme put to work upon the complexities of experience has its own peculiar range of sensations to offer: in its interactions with the other components of the poetic text it allows us to watch order emerging from, and disappearing into, disorder; it keeps us aware of the bafflements and cross-currents of creative thinking; and the rhyme-words themselves, belonging to two families at once, each with its distinctive rules of kinship, remind us that our scanning, systematising skills operate, even in the contemplation of achieved works of art, upon diverse and intractable stuff.

Some impression of the importance Mallarmé attaches to rhyme as a semantic instrument in 'Prose' may be gained simply from a comparative glance at the beginnings and endings of lines: in all cases except one (12.4) substantive objects or notions (or their actions or attributes) appear at the line-ending, whereas the lines more often than not *begin* with particles – that is to say with mere indications of relationship. No place is found for the more spectacular forms of enjambement by which, in certain of the shorter poems in octosyllables or hepta-syllables, the particles emerge into unaccustomed prominence:

> Tourbillon de mousseline ou
> Fureur éparses en écumes
> Que soulève par son genou
> Celle même dont nous vécûmes[91]

> Par son chant reflété jusqu'au
> Sourire du pâle Vasco.[92]

> Atteste quelque cigare
> Brûlant savamment pour peu
> Que la cendre se sépare
> De son clair baiser de feu[93]

In 'Prose' our attention is so often and so firmly drawn, as the line proceeds, from relationships to sensible or intelligible things that an important rhythm is created: we come to regard the line-ending as the place *par excellence* where things happen and meanings accrue.[94]

As we have already seen, the phonetic sameness of the rhyming units invites us to inspect these units for semantic affinity and involves us in the twin mental activities Hopkins called 'comparison for likeness' sake' and 'comparison for unlikeness' sake'.[95] The general structure of Mallarmé's argument is a favourable one for such comparison. It is built upon several crucial, recurrent antitheses: the same elementary binary scheme opposes the ideal and sensible worlds, the inner and outer worlds, the poet's two selves, his two modes of feeling, his two kinds of creativity. But rhyme exerts its power not simply by reinforcing oppositions which are already articulate in the poem but by presenting the fact of oppositeness or equivalence in an unusually explicit form. With four significant exceptions Mallarmé's nouns, verbs, adjectives and adverbs are used once each (the exceptions are *sœur*, *porter*, *nom* and *trop*). Although the argument takes many backward glances as it unfolds, new words and phrases are preferred to simple repetition. The argument is clarified because these are easily recognised as reformulations of what has gone before, but at the same time complicated by the new associative fields which are thereby brought into play. This means that the poem is supported on an involved and precarious framework of near-identities (a) and near-polarities (b):

(a)	(b)
sœur: enfant	science: extase
paysage: pays	soin: ampleur
île: pays	île: rive
patience: soin	atlas: paysage
hymne: œuvre	herbiers: jardin
ère d'autorité : esprit de litige	rituels: extase
	fleur: jardin

It is in a context built up in this way, by marginal variation and overlapping between the leading notions of the poem, that Mallarmé's rhymes achieve their extraordinary bite, their positive and palpable organising power. There are no rhymes in the poem which bring together pairs of synonyms or antonyms. Nowhere are phonetic equivalences crudely superimposed upon semantic ones. Mallarmé's monumental rich rhymes, precisely by being imperfect conceptual symmetries, leave the reader with work to do. They produce their clinching effect by compelling us to acts of creative, speculative participation in the unfolding of the poem.[96]

In order to illustrate the imaginative richness of individual rhymes, I have chosen two from among many relevant cases.

Consider first the rhyme *spirituels : rituels* (2). The quatrain as a whole is concerned, as I have said, with the contrast between spirituality proper and the circuitous performances and ceremonies by which the poetic mind seeks to gain access to the spiritual sphere. If the rhyme words were read alone, the second might appear to enact a loss or impoverishment of spirit: the second word may be formed by subtracting from the first, mere 'ritual' being all that remains when the defining marks of the '*spi*ritual' have been removed.[97] But during the act of reading rhymes are not available to us in this purified form. The word 'rituels' is also part of another, more plainly climactic, assertion of equivalence (*atlas : herbiers : rituels*) and thus marks a point of tension between the rhyme and syntactic axes. Two distinct implications ('ritual is loss', 'ritual is a creative necessity') are here being presented to us simultaneously, and are each to be explored later in the poem.

My other example is the first rhyme of 8 (*désir, Idées : des iridées*). In the first unit impulse and goal are separate; desire tends towards, but does not attain, its ideal objects. In the second unit the central pause has been removed and a phonetic continuum established. At the same time the distinction between tending towards and having has been dissolved: within the botanical family the realm of spirit has achieved its humanly perceivable form, and transcendent desire its fulfilment. Thus certain of the larger senses of the poem find their briefest and most concentrated formulation at the line-ending. But although the simplified conceptual models which rhyme provides draw their meaning from the argument in which the rhyme-words occur, they in turn exert their own pressure. For rhymes, by presenting as instantaneous and unqualified those relationships which within the syntactic sequence are presented gradually and with caution, compel us to re-read the argument and reappraise its rules of procedure. Rhyme has the power both to confirm and to disrupt syntax.

Although the rhymes considered individually are among the principal delights of the poem, they seem to me to represent a still greater achievement in their corporate action. The rhymes work together in two ways. Before describing these, however, I shall mention some important structural details. In nearly all cases of ultra-rich rhyme spread over several words there are fewer words in the second unit than in the first. (I have come across no other poem using the *rime équivoque* in which this happens significantly more often than not.) The commonest pattern is that whereby a single word is formed by the agglutination of component sounds from two or more other words:

sais-tu	:	vêtu
motif on dit	:	approfondit
de visions	:	devisions
se para	:	sépara
de voir	:	devoir
monotone ment	:	étonnement
par chemins	:	parchemins
sépulcre ne rie	:	Pulchérie

In *no* instance of perfect homophony are there more words on the second occasion, although there is one instance of rhyme plus additional alliteration in which the familiar pattern is reversed: *litige* : *la tige* (10). In the one case where the number of words is the same: *désir, Idées* : *des iridées*, the second unit, unlike the first, is a phonetic continuum. Thus in rhyme after rhyme the many are audibly reduced to the one. In all cases of perfect correspondence, and in all but one of imperfect (*litige* : *la tige*, again), the second rhyme unit also reduces a relatively complex rhythmic pattern to a relatively simple one. The second is therefore phonetically a repetition and rhythmically a contraction of the first. The advent of a smoother and more tightly knit unit on each second occasion could strike the reader as an unfortunate lapse from rhythmic vitality and one which the poet is unwise to repeat often. But the complaint is difficult to justify. For in a poem where other and more powerful determinants of meaning so often function in staggered and discontinuous patterns this double resolution of plurality to unity is more likely to appear as an achieved simplicity, as a concentration of purpose regained in the face of distraction.

Mallarmé is always sensitive to, and adept at exploiting, the ambiguities of natural language. Yet the fact that words are semantic units without being phonetic units, that *in sight* is indistinguishable from *incite* or *a semblé* 'from *assemblé* by phonetic analysis alone,[98] clearly exerted a special fascination in the composition of this poem. By constantly reminding his reader that identical sounds can have different meanings or grammatical status, he establishes an entire range of counter-suggestion within the poem: the very notions that the analytic elements of 'Prose' display in their tragic remoteness are shown to have a natural proximity. The poet does no more than remove a space between words and an entire metaphysical dimension changes. This mere elision of space takes on a special dramatic force in a poem which is in so many other ways concerned with the contrast between minuteness of cause and hugeness of effect.

A further aspect of rhyme gives the second half of the poem its own distinctive counterpoint. Quatrains 8–14 have always struck me as sounding more plainly triumphant than their circumspect, self-embedding sentence patterns and much qualified profession of faith could, by themselves, warrant. And a close look at rhyme goes a long way towards explaining this. (The rhyme-axis is, if anything, more prominent in the second half of the poem: the initial particles which I mentioned earlier as drawing our attention to rhyme occur more frequently than in the first half and, unprecedentedly, on eight consecutive occasions in quatrains 11 and 12.) I count 17 out of a total of 28 rhymes which allow fruitful semantic comparison between the terms. In the first half of the poem nearly all such rhymes receive from the Idealist argument a negative valuation. From each act of comparison the 'bad thing' – that which attenuates or defers the perception of the Ideal – emerges reinforced, whether by being presented twice in analogous terms:

> science : patience
> de visions : devisions

or as the second and dominant term in an antithesis:

spirituels : rituels
se para   : sépara

In the second half, on the other hand, nearly all such rhymes present opposite notions and on all occasions except one (*de voir : devoir*) the positive element is placed second:

litige   : la tige
pleure la rive : ampleur arrive
monotone ment   : étonnement
par chemins   : parchemins
sépulcre ne rie : Pulchérie
aïeul   : glaïeul

Thus these rhymes not only present the fact of polarity much more clearly than the earlier ones, but also regularly leave the sound and sense of the 'good thing' – that which promotes the perception of the Ideal – uppermost in our minds. Victory is repeatedly foretold in miniature even as the anxious contest between doubt and certainty proceeds.[99]

How agreeable it would be to leave the matter here, to say simply that as the poem moves forward the rhymes give us more and more reasons for believing that the truth Mallarmé seeks is one and indivisible: after all, multiplicity turns to unity as we read, and discontinuity to continuity, vacuum to plenum, negative to positive. How can a sense of wholeness so many times, and in so many ways, rediscovered do other than console us?

The problem lies in the atmosphere of linguistic play that I remarked upon earlier, and that is more conspicuous in Mallarmé's rhymes than anywhere else in the poem. What have word-games to do with the pursuit of the Ideal? The games have of course their poetic power. The false etymologies which Mallarmé's rhymes suggest are an affront to philology yet at the same time plausible and pertinent as imaginative constructions. The two *par/chemins* of 13 come from different places in Europe – the one from Gaul and the other from Greece[100] – and have no common semantic elements. Yet the odd adverbial phrase *par chemins* tells us a good deal about parchments: it suggests something of the problems involved in hunting them down, or deciphering them, or collating them with other documents in the establishment of a historical case. These are comparable to the poetic etymologies which crowd the pages of *Finnegans Wake* (*voyoulence*, *massoeurse*, and so forth[101]). But the imaginative operations required of us by the two writers are quite different. Joyce gives us the bundle and it's up to us to unpack it. Mallarmé gives us the components and it's up to us to make the bundle. He encourages us in the pleasures of knowingness as we watch disparate materials click, falsely and misleadingly, into place. And once he even insinuates a genuine etymology among the fanciful ones: the two *pas* in 12 are not simply homonyms but the same word *passus* in separate re-incarnations. This malicious tampering with the linguistic machine would pose no problem at all, would be a source simply of imaginative delight, if the very usefulness and integrity of language were not radically called into question in the poem. In a work where silence or, failing silence, an austere, sybilline economy of utterance are in turn put forward as the appropriate responses to transcendent vision, word-play is likely to seem frivolous and distracting. Looked at in one way the language of the poem, in its moments of spontaneous coalescence, in its sudden magical eliminations of disparity, suggests unwilled, intuitive seizure of the Ideal. But looked at – or listened to – in another way it provides no more than an idle, tinkling pageant, a moving toy-shop to which the imagination has recourse when its higher goals have, through lack of faith or energy, been abandoned.

XII

Before summarising my argument and setting forth my con-clusions, I shall return to the question, left in suspense at an early stage in this chapter,[102] of 'Prose' as a Platonic poem. In constructing this debate on the existence of the Ideal realm, Mallarmé not only treats a metaphysical issue that the Platonic tradition had been pre-eminent in perpetuating, but uses a method for articulating the issue that is itself akin to Plato's. I am here thinking of Plato more as a dramatic writer than as a simple dialectician. In a number of dialogues, of course, the essence of the debate takes place within the mind of Socrates, his interlocutors offering no more than token expressions of puzzlement, assent or approbation. But elsewhere – in the *Protagoras*, the *Gorgias*, the *Phaedrus* or the opening section of the *Parmenides*, for example – the debate is carried on between individualised minds which work with or against each other under properly dramatic conditions of uncertainty. A particularly fine instance of Plato's 'drama of ideas' is to be found towards the end of the *Phaedo* (84D–99D): Simmias and Cebes both express reservations about the proofs just given by Socrates for the immortality of the soul, and suggest alternative theories of considerable subtlety; Socrates recapitulates each theory in turn and proceeds in the light of these objections to refashion and extend his original arguments. The differences between Mallarmé's dramatic method and Plato's are plain and need not be dwelt on: the voices in Mallarmé's dialogue enter not singly but *stretto*; by means of countless fusions and displacements of sense each voice is in contact with the others and thereby acquires an additional and often problematic resonance; the poem although broadly dialectical in its movement is not dialectically resolved. But in its intellectual trenchancy, in its sure analytic grasp of difference and oppositeness, 'Prose' is a worthy successor to the dialogues. In Mallarmé's debate, as in the majority of Plato's, the ideas that matter most are those that grow from the intimately human concerns of the participants. And Mallarmé has Plato's precious capacity to round upon his own cherished notions and expose them to criticism.

My second point of contact between the two writers lies in the circumspect attitude which both at moments take towards their 'otherworldly' edifices. Although the essentials of Plato's theory of Ideas are easily compressed into a few lines of bald summary, we should remember that this theory emerges gradually in the dialogues,[103] changes its structure and is presented on a number of occasions as stubbornly problematic; most of the major questions which have, since Aristotle, exercised critics and expositors of the theory were already raised by Plato himself. Many of the difficulties are examined or touched upon in rapid succession at the beginning of the *Parmenides* (127E–136E). What is the relationship between the Ideas and the sensible world? How many Ideas are there? – one for each sensible thing? one for each genus or species? Are there Ideas of lowly or worthless things? Are Ideas in minds, the products of thought, or do they have a separate and substantial existence of their own? Can one speak of a resemblance between an Idea and a sensible thing, or are comparisons possible merely within each of the two worlds considered alone? Which mental faculties equip us to know the Ideas? Can they be known at all? Parmenides's relentless problem-raising is directed not only against Plato's teaching elsewhere, but also, in the later part of the dialogue, against the views of the historical Parmenides himself.[104] Yet although the intensity of this critical bombardment is unusual, the fact that it takes place is not: the systematic application of doubt is a necessary part of the Platonic method.

For Mallarmé the Ideas are an inexhaustibly *questionable* subject. Indeed a number of the precise issues I have just listed will at once strike the reader of 'Prose' as familiar. The crucial difference between these two interrogative performances is one of intellectual motive. Let us consider by way of example the question, common to both, whether the Ideas exist independently of our acts of thought. In my paraphrase of 'Prose' I discussed at some length the version of this question that Mallarmé raises in quatrains 3–7.[105] The answer in the *Parmenides* (132B–C) is a clear 'Yes', although this answer raises further problems.[106] The more general proposition 'the Ideas exist in us' figures in Aristotle's *Topics* (113A) as the product of an elementary piece of misreasoning; for if the Ideas existed in us then contrary predicates would necessarily belong to them: they would be both in motion and at rest, and the objects both of sensation and of thought. Mallarmé's presentation of this problem differs from *all* classical discussions in that he does not recoil from the vision of an 'impossible' world in which contrary predicates are both true. If the existence of the Ideas be granted, he is prepared to allow what the Idealist philosopher or the logician cannot: that the Ideas should be in minds and beyond minds, produced by thought but unapproachable by thought. The poem is constructed in such a way that incompatible answers to its metaphysical enquiries not only survive but necessitate each other. Mallarmé would claim for his *Idée* what Valéry claimed for his *idée fixe* in the delightful dialogue of that name: that it is *'omnivalente...S'accroche à tout...Ou: est accrochée par tout...'.*[107]

A third affinity between Plato and the Mallarmé of 'Prose', and the last that I shall mention here, concerns language. This is of such importance and complexity that a separate study would be required to do it justice; within the framework of this chapter I can provide no more than an outline of the main points.

I have examined various of the ways in which 'Prose' draws attention to itself as linguistic process – its 'reasonable' and 'unreasonable' sound figures, its whispered counter-propositions, its homonyms and its quasi-scholarly word-play. The reader who comes to 'Prose' from the dialogues will find none of this strange or incongruous. The embryonic science of etymology is called upon many times by Plato to establish the rightness or naturalness of the relationship between a name and the function performed by the person or thing bearing it.[108] Word-play, and especially poetic or whimsical etymology, is an integral part of Plato's literary manner, and used on numerous occasions in his characterisation of Socrates both as a conversational wit and as a teller of concentrated and allusive myths.[109] Moreover the *Cratylus* contains not only a compact summary of Greek thinking on language[110] but the classic formulation of a dilemma that philosophers of language have been concerned with ever since. Hermogenes maintains that the giving and using of names is a matter of convention, and Cratylus that names, by imitating the outward or essential qualities of the things to which they refer, are 'appropriate' or 'correct'. Socrates acts as arbiter in the discussion: he gives a long catalogue of imitative etymologies in apparent support of

Cratylus (393A ff.), goes on to show that Hermogenes's conventional factors play at least an important auxiliary part in the transmission of meaning (434E–435D), and concludes that the true nature of things is in any case better approached through things themselves than through the names they bear (439B).

The recent history of the two views is fascinating. For although the conventionalism proposed by Hermogenes and decisively reformulated by Saussure in his *Cours* has become the commonplace teaching of modern linguistics,[111] a strong 'cratylist' counter-current shows no sign of abating. Roland Barthes has spoken of the latter as 'ce grand mythe séculaire qui veut que le langage imite les idées et que, contrairement aux précisions de la science linguistique, les signes soient motivés.'[112] Gérard Genette in his *Mimologiques* has examined the *Cratylus* in detail, traced several of the main stages in the development of the myth and discussed the comparable roles of Plato and Mallarmé in the elaboration of a partial or secondary version of 'cratylism'.[113] Although Mallarmé's linguistics is, when abstractly formulated, firmly in the tradition of Hermogenes, he sees clearly that the goals of poetry can be served only by stepping outside the conventionalist's wisdom. In his 'Crise de vers', for example, he laments that verbal signs are imperfectly or inconsistently motivated – that *jour* and *nuit* each possess a sonority more appropriate to the other's meaning – but envisages the task of poetic language as precisely that of correcting this state of affairs: '[le vers] philosophiquement rémunère le défaut des langues.'[114] 'Prose' is by far Mallarmé's most vigorous exercise in this imaginative compensation for the deficiencies of natural language. It has the same boundless energy and inventiveness as we find in Socrates's encyclopædia of names in the *Cratylus*. And in its grandiose and semantically charged rhymes it takes us back to the very origins of European philology: for primitive etymological analysis was not concerned with verbal change and development, but proceeded as Mallarmé proceeds, simply by bringing together two phonetically similar words and allowing each to explain and motivate the other.[115] In 'Prose' Mallarmé's philological jesting keeps the entirely serious question 'what can language do?' in the forefront of the reader's mind, and teases him with glimpses into a world where the proper answer to that question is 'everything'.

XIII

Let me remind you briefly of my main propositions; I shall give them as a list. The argument of the poem is difficult. The tone in which it is conducted is often equivocal. The syntax is such as to oblige the reader to remain aware of the speculative mental processes which underlie negations and assertions, and to be speculative himself. The verse-elements in the poem do not consistently cooperate with the syntactic system, but divert the reader's attention towards many lateral relationships of affinity and contrast between syntactically remote areas of the text. Assonance, alliteration and homonymy sometimes individualise and strengthen semantic components of the text, sometimes suggest contrary meanings and sometimes appear to be in competition with meaning as such and striving towards a purely phonetic coherence. Rhyme is a strong organising principle: it keeps us aware that experience is orderable, and that diffuse and entangled notions can be simplified by the analogy-making operations of intelligence; it enacts the discovery of certainty long before argument or declared belief have established that the mind is equipped to make that discovery. But rhyme, in common with the other verse-elements, reminds us too that language can take on a deceptive substantiality of its own; that it can play us false and deter us from the quest for transcendence or for workaday clarity of mind.

I hope it is clear from what I have been saying that Proust's 'thought and metrics' and Valéry's 'semantic and phonetic variables'[116] cannot be seen in 'Prose pour des Esseintes' as harmoniously matched or impeccably interlocking. Each system works within itself according to a variety of principles; each has too many of its own internal conflicts and contradictions to enter into smooth and sustained alignment with the others.

However, my remarks have not been intended to suggest that difficulties and vexations await the reader in every corner of the poem, or that the parts of the poem randomly push and jostle each other.

My purpose has been to suggest that the poem can be read at its richest only if we are prepared to accept it as difficult and to allow that its array of concurrent and contrapuntally interwoven meanings cannot be subdued within a single allegorical frame or a single self-consistent argument. There will be moments in our reading when verse structure and syntactic structure will come apart and when one or other will take on a clearly dominant role. But in general our reading will take place *between* these systems and will have as its task the working out of a third intermediate system by which their complex interactions can be organised and articulated. In essence this is not difficult to do. For certain elementary principles are at work at all levels of the poem: we can ask the same sorts of question, apply the same sorts of test, whether we are scanning the relations between sounds, or between rhythms, or between sentences, or between metaphysical postulates: sameness or difference, simultaneity or sequence, continuity or discontinuity, contradiction or confirmation, analogy or polarity. In transferring our attention from one system to another we remain conscious of the common system-building principles which underlie both and we are able to construct all manner of bridges and staircases between them. Lower-level patterns tangibly foreshadow higher-level patterns; but there is no question of the levels being arranged in a rigorous hierarchy. We do not move by slow degrees from the 'lower' world of mere sound-effect to the 'higher' world of Spirit. The journey from phonetics to metaphysics may take place by sudden imaginative levitation: the difference between phoneme and phoneme in the outer fringes of a rhyme may suddenly be connected with, or seem but a local instance of, the very principle by which the world of sensory appearance is separated from the realm of the Ideal forms.

Mallarmé writes in the second quatrain:

> ...j'installe, par la science,
> L'hymne des cœurs spirituels

But he presents in the poem two distinct kinds of *science* – the word is appropriate in its strict sense –, and two sets of conditions in which knowledge may be pursued. According to the one view, science is essentially a taxonomic or classificatory enterprise, seeking to embrace like things within classes and classes within a hierarchy. The Ideal realm itself sanctions this: the absolute is figured not as a single flower, nor even as a genus, but as a botanical family – the *iridées* (*iridaceae*) – of which three genera are named : *iris, lis* and *glaïeul*.[117] The Ideal is envisaged as a place of different but perfectly comparable and classifiable things. At many points in the poem and notably in rhyme we can feel a confident classifying intelligence at work. But the other science is a different matter altogether; it takes place in a dangerous, intractable and often acausal world: a scandalous place in which similar causes produce dissimilar effects; in which language cannot be relied upon; in which the sound of words now enhances sense, now disrupts it. Knowledge acquired in this world is acquired against the odds, and is subject to endless revision and reformulation. Mallarmé makes us feel in our nerves the problems of knowledge and the problems of language. We feel language shifting its frames of reference as we read, catching itself out, coming up with its own refutation, proposing and counter-proposing within a single syntactic sequence.

'Too large a generalisation', Whitehead wrote, 'leads to mere barrenness. It is the large generalisation, limited by a happy particularity, which is the fruitful conception.'[118] Mallarmé's poem sets forth certain large generalisations borrowed, as I said at the start, from the Western intellectual heritage. But they are accompanied in the poem by an extraordinary limiting and vivifying array of particulars. The Ideal is constantly being checked against the sensible world, the consolingly abstract against the disconcertingly concrete. It is in the world between systems, between sciences, between 'otherworldliness' and 'this-worldliness' that Mallarmé's superbly feeling intelligence finds its proper scope.

XIV

I am affected in reading 'Prose' by the sheer unlikelihood of Mallarmé's achievement: how is it that passion so intense, thinking so incisive and virtuosity so insolent and ample could have found their way into exactly this alliance? Admirers of Bach will often find themselves asking the same sort of question when listening to, say, the six-voice ricercar in the *Musical Offering*. The fact that the multitude of overlapping and intersecting structures which these works contain should continue throughout to animate and variously connect a whole range of feelings is itself a source of wonder and places such works in a small and splendid category apart.

The texture of Mallarmé's poem may be thought of as fugal, although in a strictly limited sense. The poem gains much of its structural coherence from the delicate play of its merely implicit internal relations, in the course of which a pattern may be many times suggested and many times questioned or deferred before its moment of completeness is reached. But whereas Bach's thinking in the great fugue I mentioned above is *essentially* relational – the fugue subject revealing its full expressive riches only when played against alternative versions of itself – Mallarmé is concerned to relate propositions and systems of thought which may each lay claim to philosophical adequacy in themselves. At the end of 'Prose' we may find ourselves asking questions about Mallarmé's co-present and interacting systems which would in no way be appropriate to musical structures proper. Why live between systems? Why refuse the safety of single vision? Why refuse to bring a single self-consistent train of thought to its awaited term? The very 'overlappingness' of structure which helps to create a sense of depth and plenitude in musical argument can easily, in propositional argument, appear as a lapse from decisiveness into caution, or from candour into duplicity.

Why live between systems? The question as raised by

Mallarmé in 'Prose' is uncannily difficult. Of the many answers which are available, three seem to me specially relevant to the present case. The first is given by Empson while discussing ambiguities of his seventh type (those 'which show a fundamental division in the writer's mind'):

> A contradiction of this kind may be meaningless,
> but can never be a blank; it has at least stated the
> subject which is under discussion, and has given a
> sort of intensity to it such as one finds in a gridiron
> pattern in architecture because it gives prominence
> neither to the horizontals nor to the verticals, and
> in a check pattern because neither colour is the
> ground on which the other is placed; it is at once
> an indecision and a structure... [119]

Later in the same chapter he speaks of 'the Freudian use of opposites' in poetry. This occurs

> where two things thought of as incompatible, but
> desired intensely by different systems of judgments,
> are spoken of simultaneously by words applying to
> both; both desires are thus given a transient and
> exhausting satisfaction, and the two systems of
> judgment are forced into open conflict before the
> reader. Such a process, one might imagine, could
> pierce to regions that underlie the whole structure
> of our thought; could tap the energies of the very
> depths of the mind. [120]

In this view the poetic structure is necessarily precarious, being contrived to disguise a contradiction yet at the same time drawing attention to its own pretence. When skilfully manipulated, however, such contradiction leads not to nonsense but to the beginnings of important knowledge.

For Michel Serres in his *L'Interférence* the gridiron pattern has an even greater epistemological dignity:

> ...l'invariant me paraît immédiatement accessible:
> il désigne, à nouveau, un lieu qui n'en est pas un,

une référence qui n'est pas stable, mais le pur
mouvement de traduction d'un langage dans un
autre, la pure possibilité de transporter des formes
entre des feuillets qui se recouvrent, en partie ou
totalement, qui ont égard les uns aux autres
quoique indépendants les uns des autres, la pure
possibilité d'échange, de transfert, sans référence
première ou finale, la pure possibilité d'interférence. [. . .] l'invariant, partout transporté et en
correspondance réfléchie, le long de l'échelle, est,
sans conteste, la forme même du réseau. Les choses
sont saisies dans les mailles d'un treillis législatif à
deux, trois. . . dimensions ou entrées.[121]

In this view a system becomes useful as an instrument of knowledge only when other systems intersect it; all knowledge is
chequered, provisional, on the move. But exactly these conditions of restlessness and uncertainty give the pursuit of knowledge its exhilarating power.

For Julia Kristeva, who writes at length about 'Prose' in *La
Révolution du langage poétique*, the principal drama of the poem is
in the conflict between its syntactic system and the energies of
the unconscious mind which press towards an outlet within the
phonetic substance of the text:

. . . des *suppressions* de divers constituants syntaxiques
sont compensées par la *répétition* de phonèmes ou
de groupes phoniques qui remplacent la proposition
agrammaticale ou discutable par un 'rythme' – un
dispositif sémiotique – fonctionnant comme une
nouvelle 'unité' sémiotique, non-phrastique. En
même temps, les déplacements et les condensations
qui s'opèrent à partir de ces phonèmes ou groupes
phoniques vers d'autres lexèmes du même texte ou
d'autres textes, remplace l'*univocité du sens* propre,
théoriquement, à la phrase grammaticale, par une
ambiguïté chargée qui atteint un *polymorphisme
sémantique*.[122]

This process although violently disruptive makes the text creatively and inexhaustibly multiple: 'Ce sont [...] les ressources pulsionnelles propres au système morphophonémique et phonétique de la langue qui reconstituent une *totalité ouverte*, à signification plurielle, voire *infinie*.'[123]

The three answers which I have quoted have an important feature in common. They all display what Jean-Pierre Richard has called *l'optimisme du signifiant*[124]: for each writer the interaction of systems is a guarantee of mental creativity; co-present systems within a text deflect and disrupt each other and in so doing compel us to become producers and arbiters of meaning. The three answers are complementary, and each of them tells us something important about Mallarmé's poem. 'Prose' is contradictory and, in its contradictions, illuminates a fundamental mechanism of mind. It is disruptive and, in its disruptions, creative. It is plural and constantly in process.

And yet. . . how slender the partition is between semantic plenitude and semantic vacancy. The minutest change of perspective may bring the cessations of the poem into terrifying prominence. Only disconnect, the poet may suddenly seem to be saying. The optimistic, multiple poem may vanish as we read, and an aggressively self-cancelling poem take its place. This risk could have been avoided. But Mallarmé has chosen not only to run the risk but to spell it out among his themes. The poem ends on a note of creative affirmation beyond which other notes – those of intellectual defeat and bodily death – continue to sound.

CHAPTER THREE

Un Coup de dés jamais n'abolira le hasard

Palabras, palabras desplazadas y mutiladas, palabras de otros, fué la pobre limosna que le dejaron las horas y los siglos.
BORGES: *El Aleph*

UN COUP DE DÉS

JAMAIS

QUAND BIEN MÊME LANCÉ DANS DES CIRCONSTANCES
ÉTERNELLES

DU FOND D'UN NAUFRAGE

SOIT
    que

        l'Abîme

blanchi
    étale
       furieux
           sous une inclinaison
             plane désespérément

                 d'aile

              la sienne
                   par

avance retombée d'un mal à dresser le vol
et couvrant les jaillissements
coupant au ras les bonds

très à l'intérieur résume

l'ombre enfouie dans la profondeur par cette voile alternative

jusqu'adapter
à l'envergure

sa béante profondeur en tant que la coque

d'un bâtiment

penché de l'un ou l'autre bord

LE MAÎTRE

surgi
  inférant

de cette conflagration

que se

comme on menace

l'unique Nombre qui ne peut pas

hésite
cadavre par le bras
plutôt
que de jouer
en maniaque chenu
la partie
au nom des flots

un

naufrage cela

hors d'anciens calculs
où la manœuvre avec l'âge oubliée

jadis il empoignait la barre

à ses pieds
de l'horizon unanime

prépare
s'agite et mêle
au poing qui l'étreindrait
un destin et les vents

être un autre

Esprit
pour le jeter
dans la tempête
en reployer la division et passer fier

écarté du secret qu'il détient

envahit le chef
coule en barbe soumise

direct de l'homme

sans nef
n'importe
où vaine

ancestralement à n'ouvrir pas la main
crispée
par delà l'inutile tête

legs en la disparition

à quelqu'un
ambigu

l'ultérieur démon immémorial

ayant
de contrées nulles
induit
le vieillard vers cette conjonction suprême avec la probabilité

celui
son ombre puérile
caressée et polie et rendue et lavée
assouplie par la vague et soustraite
aux durs os perdus entre les ais

né
d'un ébat
la mer par l'aïeul tentant ou l'aïeul contre la mer
une chance oiseuse

Fiançailles

dont
le voile d'illusion rejailli leur hantise
ainsi que le fantôme d'un geste

chancellera
s'affalera

folie

N'ABOLIRA

COMME SI

Une insinuation

au silence

dans quelque proche

voltige

simple

enroulée avec ironie
                ou
                    le mystère
                            précipité
                                  hurlé

tourbillon d'hilarité et d'horreur

autour du gouffre
                    sans le joncher
                            ni fuir

                et en berce le vierge indice

                                          COMME SI

plume solitaire éperdue

sauf

que la rencontre ou l'effleure une toque de minuit
et immobilise
au velours chiffonné par un esclaffement sombre

cette blancheur rigide

dérisoire

        en opposition au ciel
   trop
     pour ne pas marquer
          exigüment
             quiconque

prince amer de l'écueil

s'en coiffe comme de l'héroïque
irrésistible mais contenu
par sa petite raison virile
                   en foudre

soucieux
    expiatoire et pubère

              muet

             La lucide et seigneuriale aigrette
                au front invisible
            scintille
               puis ombrage
          une stature mignonne ténébreuse
            en sa torsion de sirène

         par d'impatientes squames ultimes

rire

   que

SI

de vertige

debout

   le temps
       de souffleter
bifurquées

      un roc

   faux manoir
          tout de suite
              évaporé en brumes

            qui imposa
                une borne à l'infini

C'ÉTAIT
issu stellaire

CE SERAIT
pire

non

davantage ni moins

indifféremment mais autant

LE NOMBRE

EXISTÂT-IL
autrement qu'hallucination éparse d'agonie

COMMENÇÂT-IL ET CESSÂT-IL
sourdant que nié et clos quand apparu
enfin
par quelque profusion répandue en rareté
SE CHIFFRÂT-IL

évidence de la somme pour peu qu'une
ILLUMINÂT-IL

LE HASARD

Choit
la plume
rythmique suspens du sinistre
s'ensevelir
aux écumes originelles
naguères d'où sursauta son délire jusqu'à une cime
flétrie
par la neutralité identique du gouffre

RIEN

de la mémorable crise
ou se fût
l'événement

accompli en vue de tout résultat nul
                          humain

                    N'AURA EU LIEU
              une élévation ordinaire verse l'absence

                                          QUE LE LIEU
inférieur clapotis quelconque comme pour disperser l'acte vide
                        abruptement qui sinon
                            par son mensonge
                                eût fondé
                            la perdition

dans ces parages
              du vague
                    en quoi toute réalité se dissout

EXCEPTÉ
à l'altitude
PEUT-ÊTRE
aussi loin qu'un endroit

fusionne avec au delà

         hors l'intérêt
       quant à lui signalé
              en général
selon telle obliquité par telle déclivité
              de feux

   vers
     ce doit être
       le Septentrion aussi Nord

                UNE CONSTELLATION

     froide d'oubli et de désuétude
            pas tant
            qu'elle n'énumère
      sur quelque surface vacante et supérieure
          le heurt successif
                sidéralement
      d'un compte total en formation

veillant
    doutant
       roulant
        brillant et méditant

              avant de s'arrêter
        à quelque point dernier qui le sacre

         Toute Pensée émet un Coup de Dés

I

A ship, a captain, a storm; a disaster in prospect, a desperate bid, a distant hope: certain components of this extraordinary work register quickly as we begin to read. But our early attempts to gain an overall sense of the work may easily come to nothing. We may find ourselves floundering among incompatible readings, or find the poem haunted by a deconstructing demon, a scrambling device by which our successive hypotheses are made to seem paltry or disreputable even before they have been clearly formulated. Confidence in oneself as sensemaker may dwindle and disappear as guess follows ineffectually upon guess: 'There has been a disaster and mighty human energies have failed to forestall it. Or rather, a disaster is occurring now, and the human powers which until recently had seemed able and ready to prevent it are proving to be worthless. Or rather, a disaster might occur at any moment and will be prevented, if at all, by a small but decisively human intervention in the course of events...by a prudent calculation perhaps, or a blind gamble. Or at least some crisis is in question and the human capacity to respond to crisis is somehow also involved. Or at the very least something is wrong somewhere. Or, keeping our prior assumptions to that barest minimum without which thought cannot proceed, something is somewhere the case. Or is it...? Could it be that Mallarmé has brought off that supreme outrage against art, a work which means less as we read it more?'

Un Coup de dés may strike the newcomer as a text which

hesitates before its first and plainest obligation towards him: that it should have a design, a direction and something – even if it be the difficulties and embarrassments of saying – to say. Indeed it may strike him as the invention of one who is determined to withdraw rather than propose subject-matter, divert rather than pursue narrative, qualify and constrict rather than enforce his abstract pronouncements. For sentences are resolutely broken into particles. Negatives are supplanted by further negatives. Propositions lose weight while parentheses gain it. Each phrase is potentially a centre around which others may be construed, and potentially too a far semantic periphery beyond which nonsense and hubbub reign. Print suddenly gives pattern to the space which surrounds it, and is as suddenly scattered by that same space become mobile and aggressive. French is being translated into an unknown language. Here is an exercise in reading which requires of us that we unlearn to read, a mode of discourse where the answers to questions are questions, where dilemmas resolved are dilemmas still, and where the very notion of intelligibility appears to be under threat.

Look at the poem, as a still-puzzled newcomer, in one way and you will find a number of imperfectly superimposed sign-systems – language, variable type-faces and spacing, pictorial imitation – which seem capable of producing indefinitely many momentary structures: the systems traverse and coerce each other so intensively that we are left with the impression not of system but of teeming accidental detail. But look at it in another way and many of these details begin to add up and to point in a single direction – that of an unthinkable blankness lying beyond the busy textures of the poem. It is now as if Mallarmé were edging us into a realm where, beyond the local, chance-governed complexities of experience, a terrifying obviousness lies in wait for us and where minds fail because nothing remains to be perceived, or understood, or cherished, or repudiated. The text seems to be unstable in itself and inconsistent in the demands it makes upon us as readers: at one moment every-thing in it matters, all its features tell, and the next moment nothing matters except the world without feature which it compels us to view.

Many of these initial perplexities are in fact cleared up as we read the poem more closely. We are soon able to define the broad range of sensations and issues that Mallarmé is concerned with, and to name with conviction certain things which the poem is *not about*. We learn to discriminate between main and subordinate materials, to disentangle subjects from predicates and to piece together arguments, aetiologies, chronologies and narrative structures with which to keep provisional order in the text as we set out to re-read it. But although we are unlikely to relive at any later stage the full panic of our early readings, some sense of intellectual and emotional insecurity is likely to remain a permanent element in our response to *Un Coup de dés*. It is the least relaxing of Mallarmé's works. And at any stage in our acquaintance with it, we must be prepared to find that our latest reading discredits rather than confirms the one that went before.

II

Mallarmé read this poem to Valéry shortly after its completion. Valéry was surprised by what he heard and still more surprised by what he then saw:

> Il me sembla de voir la figure d'une pensée, pour
> la première fois placée dans notre espace... Ici,
> véritablement, l'étendue parlait, songeait, enfantait
> des formes temporelles. L'attente, le doute, la
> concentration étaient *choses visibles*. Ma vue avait
> affaire à des silences qui auraient pris corps[...] Je
> me sentais livré à la diversité de mes impressions,
> saisi par la nouveauté de l'aspect, tout divisé de
> doutes, tout remué de développements prochains.
> Je cherchais une réponse au milieu de mille
> questions que je m'empêchais de poser. J'étais un
> complexe d'admiration, de résistance, d'intérêt
> passionné, d'analogies à l'état naissant, devant cette
> invention intellectuelle.[1]

Ever since this exemplary first encounter between *Un Coup de dés* and its readership, the look of the poem on the page has produced reactions of astonishment and, in many cases, of distrust. Even as our eyes stray over the text before we resolve to read, it is clear that *Un Coup de dés* has broken many of the tacit agreements upon which the act of reading rests. The poem has designs upon us, puts us on our guard, compels us to take up a position. We are perplexed by the empty stretches of paper and indignant, perhaps, that the author's intentions in thus disturbing our received notions of the poem and the book have not been fully declared.

The inscrutability of *Un Coup de dés*, and the abruptness of its challenge to literate intelligence, have been little diminished by the traditions of typographical experiment and verbal randomisation which have grown up in the years since its composition. Some acquaintance with the *calligrammes* of Apollinaire, the ideograms and jagged lineation of Pound's *Cantos*, or such 'poem-objects' as Raymond Queneau's *Cent mille milliards de poèmes* and Jacques Roubaud's ∈ will of course help to create an appropriate frame of mind in which to read Mallarmé's poem – a frame of mind in which we expect typographically unusual poems to be unusually plural and relativised in their meanings. But no subsequent work provides even a remotely useful explanatory model for this one. Indeed no poem that I know of from any age so firmly forbids the eye or mind to alight upon it and be still. Why are the words scattered upon the page? The question is an insistent one, and likely to trouble the reader long after certain of those words have been sufficiently contracted or regrouped to form cogent statements.

An entire range of answers with which criticism has been much occupied proposes that the poem is fashioned upon the page in imitation of its subject matter.[2] These answers are simple and convenient, and have the approval of tradition. After all, George Herbert's 'The Altar' is altar-shaped and his 'Easter-Wings' wing-shaped; the mouse in *Alice* tells a tail-shaped tale; and the gradually increasing and decreasing line-lengths of 'Les Djinns', Hugo's masterpiece of *terribilità*, trace upon the page an elementary dynamics of nightmare. *Un Coup de dés* contains two main, interpenetrating vocabularies: these concern, on the one hand, seafaring, tempest and shipwreck and, on the other, the pursuit of knowledge and the attempt to define the mental or metaphysical conditions by which that pursuit is deflected, discredited or annulled. The sea vocabulary readily suggests ways in which the page may be read as a rudimentary set of pictorial signs: here are a tilting deck, a plunging prow, a toppled mast (if one cares to distinguish the details of the drama) or a general litter of driftwood (if one is impatient with niceties or nautically untutored). Readers who take an epistemological view of the poem have a slightly more difficult task. The unusually large spaces which interrupt all statements except the last may be seen to represent either the impediments to clear thinking with which the mind contends from moment to moment, or that threat of final and unanswerable nullity which no act of thought, for Mallarmé, completely dispels. In this way the poem may be seen as a portrait of thought at risk, an 'inscape' of the anxious and intellectually questing mind.

I have little to quarrel with in these mimetic accounts of *Un Coup de dés*, except where they actively trivialise or coarsen Mallarmé's text. But none of them takes us far in the understanding of that text, and nearly all seriously understate the semantic functions which variable spacing and type-faces serve. (These functions are outlined with admirable trenchancy by Mallarmé in his preface to the poem[3].) The visual devices are but one among the many jointly operative procedures by which meaning is created and transformed. Although visual pattern-seeking is a necessary part of the continuous speculative activity in which the text involves us, the patterns have little imaginative power in themselves: the pictorial sign-system is too little developed to be able fully to collaborate or fully to conflict with its extraordinarily intricate verbal counterpart. It is exactly this calculated unbalance which removes Mallarmé's text – like those of Herbert and Hugo – from the sphere of concrete poetry.[4] For the concrete or 'calligrammatical' poet seeks to superimpose sign-systems upon each other with a view to the construction of a more or less elegant and ironically suggestive tautology. He attempts to evolve a language which will be at the same time alphabetic and hieroglyphic; and in order to curtail the advantage which the alphabet traditionally enjoys in the West, and thereby preserve parity between the two modes, he often restricts his alphabetic message to the simplest of statements (as in Apollinaire's 'Il Pleut'[5]) or to isolated words (as in Pierre Garnier's 'Soleil mystique'[6]). Mallarmé's bias is plain: he sides so firmly with the alphabet and with syntax that the moment of tautology between systems is indefinitely postponed. Pictorial meanings provide no more than a tenuous tracery of suggestion around his startling syntactic scheme.

By far the most fruitful way of envisaging the spaces of *Un Coup de dés* is as a set of diacritical marks, of instructions or hints on how to read the words of the poem.[7] This approach raises its own problems. For even if the reader takes a limited view of these instructions and regards them as governing solely such matters as stress and tempo, he will feel entitled by the visual character of the poem to disregard these quasi-musical indications whenever he chooses: each double page may be read 'forwards' (in which case these indications apply) or with an irregular, exploratory movement of the eye (in which case they do not).

The causes of this uncertainty may be tracked down to the smallest details of Mallarmé's spacing. Let us consider two straightforward cases:

> dans ces parages / du vague / en quoi toute
> réalité se dissout   (10)
>
> veillant / doutant / roulant / brillant et méditant (11)

In both examples, the large spaces correspond with conventional semantic breaks and are extensions of those we would expect to find in everyday written French. But whereas the sub-units of the first phrase are grammatically discrete, those of the second are grammatically equivalent. With an identical gesture, that is, Mallarmé dramatises on the one occasion difference and on the other sameness. If in the majority of the remaining cases the syntax of the poem were as clear as in these, both functions of space could subsist without interfering with each other. Indeed the clear logical relationship – that of contrariety – which exists between the two meanings could make the space-sign more useful, just as the same relationship guards against rather than encourages misunderstanding in such well-known cases of 'acceptable' polysemy as *altus* (meaning both 'high' and 'deep') or *hôte* ('host' and 'guest').

But the syntax is seldom as clear as in the examples I quoted. However vividly we bear the simple test-cases in mind as we approach a new and unexplained blank segment of page, the lessons of experience tell us no more than 'this space is either a "stop" or a "go"': the sentence, clause or phrase you are reading either finishes here or continues'. Thus on (4) 'l'unique Nombre', which is the subject of the verbs *se préparer*, *s'agiter* and [*se*] *mêler*, may be qualified in one of three ways, according to the pattern of stops we choose:

l'unique Nombre qui ne peut pas

l'unique Nombre qui ne peut pas être un autre

l'unique Nombre qui ne peut pas être un autre Esprit

As we feel our way towards the neatest or the most pertinent of these readings – and this involves much long-term calculation and retracing of steps – the spaces themselves maintain an often enervating neutrality. If we are helped in our overall quest for coherence by those spaces which clearly punctuate the developing 'forwards' sense of the poem, we are made cautious again by those freaks and outliers among Mallarmé's fragments which have no claim, semantic, syntactic or metrical, to be considered alone: 'que de jouer', 'où vaine', 'ou se fût', 'pas tant' and so forth.[8] In reading spaces which have a clear 'stop' function it is often unclear which syntactic unit is being closed: noun phrases, main and subordinate clauses, sentences, parentheses and sub-parentheses all end with the same sign. These factors make it difficult to claim sensibly that Mallarmé's spaces have been provided to afford us a smooth passage through the text.

The equivocal pause is not unusual in poetry. Indeed in blank verse and free verse it might even be classed as a minor standard device. It occurs often in *Paradise Lost*:

> Cover me ye Pines,
> Ye Cedars, with innumerable boughs
> Hide me...[9]

It was ingeniously exploited by the *vers-libristes* and later became a major expressive resource in the works of Reverdy and Éluard:

> Le monde s'efface
> Au point où je disparaîtrai
> Tout s'est éteint[10]

But no poet has gone further in the manipulation of this pause than Mallarmé in *Un Coup de dés*. For every space in the poem is equivocal; it is impossible to read the text in such a way that those functions of space which are irrelevant to a given instance simply remain in abeyance while the 'correct' function is being performed. In each case we choose our reading from a range of candidates by a process of trial and error. It is preposterous to imagine that as we learn to make our choices more efficiently and so find the poem gradually settling into a more assured linear sense we are fulfilling Mallarmé's main purpose in fragmenting his text, or that the problem of the spaces will in time disappear. It would have been sheer perversity and obscurantism on Mallarmé's part to use a single ambiguous diacritical mark as an 'aid' to the proper construing of his argument when a variety of such marks, each with a clear individual meaning, would have achieved the same purpose more rapidly and with less fuss. We need not invoke Mallarmé's artistic conscience or his common sense in order to persuade ourselves that such an intention is unworthy of him: the superior imaginative power of the poem when pluralistically read is evidence enough. The spaces are two positive indications in one. They invite us not only to pause in our forwards reading but to develop another, concurrent reading method. Each fragment, isolated by space from its neighbours and its syntactic dependents, becomes available to us in new ways. It may rise clear of the remaining text with sudden formulaic insistence and, against a background of indistinct part-meanings, impress itself upon us as a complete semantic event:

la mer par l'aïeul tentant ou l'aïeul contre la mer   (5)

prince amer de l'écueil   (7)

une élévation ordinaire verse l'absence   (10)

selon telle obliquité par telle déclivité   (11)

Or it may participate in an entire network of rebellious structures which constrain and short-circuit the linear sense. For instance, the members of such series or antitheses as *ultérieur : ultime*, *puérile : pubère : virile*, *inférieur : supérieur* can easily, despite the syntactic barriers which separate them, rejoin each other to form instantaneous patterns of meaning. In the course of the asyntactic scanning which Mallarmé encourages us to perform, we may come upon structures which offer reduced models of the general arguments enacted in the text. Those I have listed are clearly of this kind. But these structures, far from simply reinforcing the larger development of the poem, suggest an alternative, synchronic mode of meaning which calls the very idea of a *developing* poem into question. I noted a tension of the same kind in discussing the rhyme-pairs of 'Prose pour des Esseintes'. Later in this chapter I shall say more about the disruptive force of these lateral structures.

I have dwelt upon the multifarious semantic texture which Mallarmé's lay-out helps to create in *Un Coup de dés* in order to show that certain hazards of interpretation may be avoided if we take that lay-out seriously. I have no wish to enter the labyrinths of wishful thinking in which a number of commentators who sought to read the poem allegorically have already been lost. This does not mean that I am out of sympathy with their desire to see the work as fundamentally simple despite its intricacies, and succinct despite its deviations and delays. But allegory serves that desire poorly. My own view is that the human problem at issue is a simple one, and that the complexities of texture through which it passes serve to broaden its intellectual and moral compass. At its crudest the allegorical approach commits the double wrong of falsely embellishing the problem and falsely normalising the texture.

III

The clearest internal route to *Un Coup de dés* is by way of the early prose tale *Igitur* and the three maritime sonnets of Mallarmé's later years, 'Salut' ('Rien, cette écume, vierge vers'), 'Au seul souci de voyager' and 'A la nue accablante tu'.[11] In *Igitur* Mallarmé's hero is by turns uplifted and oppressed by the pure, chance-defying act which it is his ancestral responsibility to perform. Such an act is indefinitely problematic. For it appears to offer a perfect release from the contingencies of physical and mental process and to procure an indissoluble identity for the mind which performs it. Yet because it is an act of repudiation, it contains within itself a reassertion of that which it is called upon to deny: in order to be cancelled chance must first exist. The following passage, summarising the major phases of the drama, contains a characteristically anxious vacillation upon this theme:

> *Bref dans un acte où le hasard est en jeu, c'est toujours le hasard qui accomplit sa propre Idée en s'affirmant ou se niant. Devant son existence la négation et l'affirmation viennent échouer. Il contient l'Absurde – l'implique, mais à l'état latent et l'empêche d'exister: ce qui permet à l'Infini d'être.*[12]

The act which seeks to disallow chance allows it still. But the realm of chance, now reaffirmed, contains within itself – within its endless multitude of potentialities – the idea of infinity; from this idea a further act of denial will spring. But that act, in turn...And so forth. In its unfinished state *Igitur* contains some abstract writing of rare brilliance, although the larger effect of these passages is muddled by much private mythology and a diffuse Gothic scenario. The main problem left unsolved by Mallarmé in *Igitur* was that of finding a concrete situation which would enforce rather than limit the generality of his theme, and a dramatic structure which would suggest the metaphysical uncertainty inherent in that theme without appearing loose and indecisive.

One of the sonnets I mentioned above was published two years before *Un Coup de dés* and represents Mallarmé's first complete solution to the problem. It is this solution which re-appears in more elaborate form in the later work:

A la nue accablante tu
Basse de basalte et de laves
A même les échos esclaves
Par une trompe sans vertu

Quel sépulcral naufrage (tu
Le sais, écume, mais y baves)
Suprême une entre les épaves
Abolit le mât dévêtu

Ou cela que furibond faute
De quelque perdition haute
Tout l'abîme vain éployé

Dans le si blanc cheveu qui traîne
Avarement aura noyé
Le flanc enfant d'une sirène.[13]

(Among the many distinctions of this work should be counted that of having drawn Tolstoy's wrath: 'This poem is not exceptional in its incomprehensibility. I have read several other poems by Mallarmé and they also had no meaning whatever.'[14]) The image of a storm-tossed ship offered several important advantages. It was well enough known to be re-specifiable in a few rapid touches; thanks to a centuries-old tradition in legend, literature and painting it was a ready-made emblem for crisis in human affairs. It suggested urgency and deadliness, and in a way that was clearly related to the conduct of ordinary lives: the fustian and the pointless appurtenances which spoiled *Igitur* have completely disappeared.

There are numerous verbal overlappings between this sonnet and *Un Coup de dés: naufrage, abîme, sirène, perdition, écume(s)*, *abolir* and *suprême* occur in both; *blanc* and *furibond* appear in the one and *blancheur, blanchir* and *furieux* in the other. The simple and magnificent question asked in the two poems is the same: is there a means of escape from the wreck of experience? In the sonnet this question takes the double form: has the siren been seen or not? (was she illusory or not?) if she has been seen, has she survived the storm? In *Un Coup de dés* it becomes: is structure ('le nombre', 'une constellation') attainable, whether by grace or by effort, by calculation or by intuition, over and against the teeming chaos of things? The syntax of the poems is of the collapsible and adjustable kind which allows each to be read both as a developing sea-drama and as a set of possible risks and possible outcomes all simultaneously in force: each poem is both an unfolding series of events and an instantaneous, manifold event. Not only does the central image suggest at once stillness and accelerated process, but it binds together and 'interinanimates' two quite distinct frames of reference, one psychological and one metaphysical; both poems are concerned equally to characterise a mental state – of panic and unknowing – and to articulate a metaphysical enquiry: what is really there in the world?

The later poem does not simply amplify the imagery of the earlier and replace regular octosyllabic metre by a more fluid system of 'spatialised' scansion. For Mallarmé introduces into *Un Coup de dés* a language of gnomic abstraction which appears rarely in his previous work and not at all in 'A la nue...'. The propositions framed in this language have a major structural role: they help us to distinguish probable from improbable messages as we pick our way through the embedded parentheses which comprise the remainder of the text. They are made immediately legible by being printed in capitals or, in the last case, as an unbroken sequence:

Un coup de dés jamais n'abolira le hasard

Rien n'aura eu lieu que le lieu, excepté peut-être une constellation

Toute pensée émet un coup de dés

(To these we might add the conditional sentence 'Si c'était le nombre ce serait le hasard' which appears on (8) and (9).) These propositions have something of the terrifying simplicity which we find in certain of the Heraclitean fragments or in Blake's 'Proverbs of Hell'.[15] They have the syntax of axioms; they concern central and unavoidable dilemmas within human experience; and they are uttered with such stern forthrightness that their challenge is all but impossible to refuse. Which would be worse, we are left wondering – that all this should be true, or that it should not?

The title-maxim may be paraphrased in a number of ways: no act of knowing eliminates the unknowable; no would-be definitive thought may free itself from contingency; no action of whatever kind may perfectly transcend the conditions of its execution. Mallarmé's reference to gaming has a special ironic grimness about it. For dice-throwers are not seekers after transcendence; to cast the dice, to play the game, is not simply to acknowledge that chance exists: it is an act of willing acquiescence in the way things are, a refusal to protest. The hidden motive of Mallarmé's utterance is clearly: would that things were otherwise and that dice-throwing *did* abolish chance. Beyond the bleakly rule-bound dice-game he refers to, he has envisaged another game the only rule of which is that no rule should apply. Within a single sentence this alternative game, which is that of the pure act, has been posited and pronounced impossible.

The final line of the poem confirms what we may well have suspected earlier: that the poem is a model of the thought-process at large and that, within the terms of this model, thought is inevitably pitched beyond itself and towards the unconditional act, the game without rules, which practical good sense condemns. Harmony prevails between the two maxims if they are removed from their context and considered together; they are the first and second stages of an elementary syllogism. But in their context they behave differently. For it is a main purpose of Mallarmé's volatile textures to give voice to the hidden motives or 'illocutionary forces' which the maxims themselves leave unspoken. The awaited third stage of the syllogism – that 'no thought will ever abolish chance' – must be the case yet cannot be granted. This, the logical outcome of Mallarmé's argument, has been shown throughout the poem to be a cause of alarm, a challenge, and a lure towards the acutest form of metaphysical risk.

Un Coup de dés is a world of alternative logics. The rules of the game are both respected and infringed as we read; the limits within which thought is obliged, or content, to operate are drawn and redrawn from moment to moment; the poet's language of axiomatic self-evidence and sequential argument is disrupted by a precarious language of feeling and surmise which is intent upon making the impossible come, at least momentarily, true. The 'impossible' chance-abolishing thought is present as a permanent temptation to which minds are subject and, in the final, culminating pages, as the only hope worth retaining amid chaos and dissolution.

Those apparent features of the world by which acts of thought are most constrained – and principally chance, contingency and randomness – play a prominent part in the poem. Indeed they are so clearly enunciated, and so clearly enacted in its disjointed syntax and its scattered distribution in space, that the opposite, redeeming notions of structure and stability may seem at first sight to have been understated. But these notions draw their power from a different source: they are stated sparingly, but at precisely those points of climax and convergence within the argument where even the smallest verbal gestures can cause a new balance of ideas to be struck (see, in particular, (9) and (11)).

Supreme among these redeeming notions is that of *number*, and Mallarmé has given it a multiple resonance far beyond anything that a mere 'allegory of the dice-thrower' might require. Since the Pythagoreans, for whom number was the complete answer to the question 'what is really there in the world?', the notion has had a special prestige.[16] In many areas of natural science, it is the sole means of ensuring that knowledge shall remain testable and transmissible. But poets have in general remained cautious. Although many of them have used numerical or numerological procedures in organising their texts, few have chosen to dignify number by taking it as a poetic theme.[17] Mallarmé in *Un Coup de dés*, far from rejecting the notion as 'unpoetic', as lying beyond the realm of discriminate feeling, calls upon it to represent the longed-for ideal of intelligible structure.

In this his reaction is quite different from Baudelaire's, who had ended 'Le Gouffre' with the lines:

Je ne vois qu'infini par toutes les fenêtres,

Et mon esprit, toujours du vertige hanté,
Jalouse du néant l'insensibilité.
– Ah! ne jamais sortir des Nombres et des Êtres![18]

The comparison is worth making because the two poems belong in other ways to the same lineage; both describe the intrusions of chaos and nonentity into the everyday operations of mind. *Numbers* for Baudelaire are part of the problem: that a seething and circumstantial world should be numerable is in itself a further cause of horror. The mind is powerless to control this realm of indefinitely multipliable quantities. *Number* (the singular form, the principle of numerability) is for Mallarmé a means of escape from the undifferentiated flood of phenomena;

it is the tenuous foretaste of knowledge, the promise of a world simplified, organised and understood. Where Baudelaire envisages his release from circumstance as a final blankness and insentience, Mallarmé envisages his as a perception of pattern. His perfect model of intelligibility takes various forms and is given various names; it is number, it is Idea and, in this celebrated cry from *La Musique et les lettres*, it is literature itself: 'Oui, que la Littérature existe et, si l'on veut, seule, à l'exception de tout.'[19]

IV

The abstract propositions in which these elliptic philosophical debates between pure act and circumstance, and between number and chance, are set forth will be felt by most readers to be concerned with the same fundamental problems as those embodied in the imagery of storm and shipwreck. But this is not a case of simple parallelism between the abstract and concrete languages of the poem. For many words are simultaneously active within both frames of reference and compel us to a special sort of mediate or transitional thinking. The word 'plume', for example, clearly belongs to Mallarmé's maritime drama: the self hovers feather-like above the scene of disaster not knowing whether to accept or to resist the threat of prompt and unredeemable extinction which the abyss appears to offer. Yet by means of this word Mallarmé alludes not only to the perilous lives of airborne creatures, but to that metaphysical gaming which is his main abstract theme: a simple and obvious association of ideas will bring the commonplace phrase 'jeter la plume au vent' (and with it the general notion of chance) into the reader's mind.

Or again, consider the word 'nombre' itself. It refers us to the science of navigation no less than to dice-games or to the general question of whether experience is numerable or structurable: just as the intelligence seeks for regularities within the arbitrary welter of phenomena, so the mariner, in order to stay afloat and on course, has to get his numbers right.

'Nombre' has a further, more delicate, intermediary role in the poem. Although rhyme proper appears seldom in *Un Coup de dés* other phonetic correspondences are prominent enough to make the reader attentive to the sound texture of the work and to its several instances of subdued, long-range word-play: *(le) voile : (la) voile; (le) vague : (la) vague; poing : point; nom : non; temps : tant : tentant.*[20] Among such cases that of 'nombre' is the most interesting. In the early stages of the poem *nombre* and *ombre* represent one of many implicit word-pairs contrasting security and danger, and are by their phonetic similarity more likely than others to be noticed. (In the poem as a whole these words are reinforced by such cognates as *calcul, se chiffrer, énumérer*, on the one hand, and *sombre, ombrager* and *minuit*, on the other.) Towards the end this contrast is suddenly and dramatically confirmed, and the logical hiatus between the words removed: on (9) 'le nombre' is conceived of ('existât-il commencât-il et cessât-il se chiffrât-il illuminât-il') as a possible source of illumination, a destroyer of shadows, and therefore as a proper and necessary negative of *ombre*: a *'non-ombre'*. But at the very point where the *nombre : ombre* polarity is made explicit, the crucial philosophical dilemma is also declared, and with an equivalent emphasis: 'si c'était le nombre ce serait le hasard'. The single word *nombre*, as it appears on (9), thus plays an extraordinary double role: its literal and metaphorical senses have been made simultaneously, yet still separately, legible.

It is difficult to talk clearly about the structure of *Un Coup de dés* without dividing it into parallel levels, the one abstract and the other concrete, the one concerned with an intellectual crisis and the other with an adventure at sea. Some such hierarchy as this is of course installed within the text by Mallarmé himself. The entire poem is laid out as a single proposition variously qualified and variously illustrated. An immediately palpable difference of tone and focus separates the short abstract pronouncements from such voluble specimens of seafarer's nightmare as: 'son ombre puérile / caressée et polie et rendue et lavée / assouplie par la vague et soustraite / aux durs os perdus entre les ais' (5). But although these levels have a clear organising function in the poem, they have a narrow interpretative use. For if we posit that *Un Coup de dés* is 'really' about randomness and structure, or about the characteristic risks of defeat and dissolution run by keenly self-scrutinising minds, and that sea, storm, hull and reef are present simply to give savour and particularity to this conceptual matter, we shall provide ourselves with a neat allegorical diagram which is hopelessly clumsy and uninformative in reading the detail of the text. Steering a ship, casting a die, thinking one's way beyond the limitations of thought – none of these activities has a 'natural' priority in the organisation of the poem; none is more elevated or broader in its human scope than the others. There is no 'natural' direction for metaphorical invention: the perils of thinking are as much a metaphor for physical danger as the other way round. The languages of the poem are indefinitely translatable and retranslatable into one another. Words such as *plume* and *nombre* – and there are many others of the same amphibious kind – do not stand at the point of easy transition between Mallarmé's separate frames of reference, but at the point where one frame intrudes upon another, pulls it out of true and imposes upon the reader the task of re-establishing order.

Un Coup de dés is an uncannily rigorous and clear-headed attempt to represent the sensations of contingency. Mallarmé takes us into a world where the distinction between mental and physical has to be fought for and does not last, and where distraction, turmoil and death are now universal and now minutely local in their scope. This is a world where ships sink, where patiently built conceptual structures collapse and where human beings despair and die. The would-be independent languages or levels of the poem, as they reinvent and redefine each other from moment to moment, yield a specially intense and unstable sort of meaning. The poem places upon us the burden of inventing its senses minutely and momentarily, and against a background now of vacancy, now of intractable multiplicity. We can escape from all this if we wish, and the allegorical subordination of 'anecdote' to 'philosophy' is an easy way of doing so. But the uniform intellectual exchange-system which such a view of the work presupposes has nothing to do with the uncertain conditions of mind in which Mallarmé's pursuit of knowledge takes place. For Mallarmé conceptual and emotional indecision is neither a morbidity of temperament nor an awkwardness of style: it is the sign of a tenacious and often painful fidelity to the facts of experience; it provides him with the raw materials from which his instruments of discovery are made.

Mallarmé knows far too much about the pleasures of sensation and about the pains and absurdities of the intellectual life to become the immaculate mind-suprematist that certain of his admirers have wished to cast him as. He sees with rare clarity how facile the mind can become in dissolving away the stubborn angularities of the physical world. And it is one of his many achievements in *Un Coup de dés* to have demonstrated some of the risks to which the self-made mentalist is exposed: not only can he provide himself with a world of stifling inanity, but wave or rock can at any moment leap back from the metaphorical shadow-realm to which he had consigned it and again become real, peremptory and lethal.

V

It is surprising enough to find that a work which is wilfully fragmented in texture should contain so much inventive dialectical thinking, and that the tragic dialogue between pure act and circumstance should be conducted with such fine gradations of irony. But it is still more surprising that this splendidly organised and overspilling portrait of contingency should be cast in a language which is dominated by negatives, privatives and limiting parentheses. By comparison with 'Prose pour des Esseintes', where the poet's several positives are forcibly articulated, and enshrined within the argument of the poem, the redeeming notions of fixity and structure are presented throughout with teasing obliqueness. They are nowhere stated even reticently as axioms. Nouns denoting turmoil, or dissolution, or emptiness by far outnumber those of any other group: *naufrage, abîme, conflagration, tempête, disparition, silence, gouffre, tourbillon, folie, vertige, délire, crise, hallucination, brumes, (le) vague, absence, mensonge, contrées nulles, résultat nul, acte vide, cime flétrie, surface vacante.* And there is no stable point of view – unless it be that of relentless philosophical doubt – from which these manifold indications of absence or loss are considered and controlled. Qualifications are interrupted so rapidly by further qualifications that the opening pages, if we transcribed them using the three conventional marks of parenthesis, might look like this:

> Un coup de dés jamais (quand bien même lancé
> dans des circonstances éternelles, du fond d'un
> naufrage, – soit que l'Abîme, blanchi, étale, furieux,
> sous une inclinaison plane désespérément d'aile
> (la sienne) par avance retombée...

As we move forward from here Mallarmé's stratified syntax has left us with three incomplete patterns and a clear invitation to pursue all three at once. How can any poem be made from breaks, from absences, from moments of unseeing and un-knowing? How can the many vacancies and discontinuities marshalled by Mallarmé in *Un Coup de dés* produce their effects of brilliance and compacted imaginative variety?

I shall briefly discuss three further features of the poem, and then in the light of them suggest how these questions can best be answered. The features I have in mind are sound-patterning, syntax and imagery, although in each case I shall limit my remarks to one or two aspects only.

The sound figures operate much less systematically, and carry correspondingly less information, than those of 'Prose'. But their contribution to the polysemantic fabric of the poem is still an important one. Figuration of the kind found in such phrases as

> l'ultérieur démon immémorial [lleʀjʀemmemʀjl]
>
> tourbillon d'hilarité et d'horreur [tʀidiʀiteedʀʀ]
>
> froide d'oubli et de désuétude [ddeddeed]

helps to give these sub-units of sentences an air of complete and often monumental statement. However the effect of like sounds in these instances is not necessarily to elucidate the sense of the words. For the words which compose each phrase are drawn from abruptly different associative fields, refashion each other's familiar senses and together have considerable power to resist the unifying effect of assonance and alliteration. The more difficulty we have in grasping the overall sense of a phrase the more readily will its corresponding sounds appear as an independent pattern: they may even suggest an abstract play of symmetries which refuses to interlock with the syntactic sequence, and the reader may find himself hesitating between two apparently divergent tendencies of the sentence.

A more pronounced flicker of uncertainty is produced in cases where sound likeness occurs both within and between adjacent fragments:

sur quelque surface vacante et supérieure
[sуʀklksуʀfskesуeʀœʀ]

le heurt successif   [lœʀsyksesif]

sidéralement   [sieʀl]

For the matching sounds join the fragments and the blank spaces quite as strongly disjoin them. The prominent series [sуʀ sуʀ sy sy si si] gives a strong backbone to a set of phrases which are presented to the eye as discontinuous. At each junction between phrases syntax and sound together issue one imperative ('continue') and spatial distribution another ('stop'). Minor hesitations of this kind would go unnoticed, or would be suppressed by the reading mind as uninstructive oddities, if the text were not organised in such a way as to suggest that hesitation is important and able to serve precise epistemological ends. As it is, the two-way pulls to be felt within the sequences I have mentioned are reminders in little of the central intellectual tensions within Mallarmé's poem.

The sound [i], which appears in such a striking assonantal display in 'Le vierge, le vivace...', contributes more variously than any other phoneme to the sound texture of *Un Coup de dés*. It is likely to be brought to our attention first by the multitude of polysyllables in which it appears either in two successive vowel positions (*division, probabilité, précipité, immobilise, rigide, irrésistible, virile, invisible, infini, rythmique, sinistre, originelles, obliquité, déclivité*) or with another vowel intervening (*inutile, disparition, ironie, hilarité, minuit, illuminât, identique*). These words form a subdued refrain of assonances extending throughout the poem. But the sound is likely to emerge from this refrain, and assume some measure of semantic power, only when other factors serve to motivate it. On certain double pages, for example, [i] appears both in the words or word-groups which are accented by capitalisation and with unusual frequency in the rest of the text. These two modes of emphasis – repetition and capital letters – reinforce one another: 'n'abolira' (5), 'comme si' (6), 'si') (8) or the series of imperfect subjunctives culminating in 'illuminât-il' (9) may echo, and be echoed in, the bulk of the page in such a way as to suggest that each is by turns cause and effect of the other. (It is worth noting that in three of the four cases I have listed the idea which is thus stressed is that of *conditionalness*.)

Furthermore this or any other repeated phoneme may act as an additional, confirming sign of uniformity in places where that idea is already present:

de l'hor*i*zon u*n*a*ni*me

Une *insin*uation / *sim*p*l*e / au *silenc*e / *en*rou*l*ée avec *i*ron*i*e

cette blancheu*r* *rigid*e / *déri*soire

p*ar* *la* neu*tral*it*é* *i*den*ti*que du gouffre

These phrases are important to the argument of the poem. Each marks a point of defeat for the discriminating intelligence; in each Mallarmé alludes to that final, unthinkable blankness in which all particulars and all identities are lost. This is the permanently threatening uniformity which each successive act of thought sets out to challenge and which provides for that act an impassable outer boundary. The reminder of sameness which this repeated [i] provides from phrase to phrase may subliminally suggest that this boundary, although approachable from many directions and with a variety of stratagems and precautions, itself does not vary. The phrases in question would suggest this even in the absence of sound-play. They are of the self-subsistent kind which easily break free from their syntactic restrictions and, even across the large expanses of text which separate them, appear as alternative versions of each other, or as a series of comparable cases all governed by some unspoken rule of thought.

The most remarkable and the most informative of these sound patterns is that special form of anagrammatic writing by which certain words, and notably those at the phrase-ending, may be cast into relief. In such cases as the following each sound of the 'key-word' or 'key-phrase' is repeated within the phrases which immediately follow it:

puérile: caress*ée* et *po*l*ie* et rend*ue* et *la*v*ée*

quand apparu: e*n*fin | *par qu*elq*ue* prof*u*sion *rép*and*ue*
en *rar*eté

flétrie: par la neu*tralité* i*den*t*i*que du gou*ffre*

nul: h*u*main | *n*'aura *eu l*ieu

While in the following the repetition is complete but for a single phonemic variation (which I give in brackets):

contrées nulles: induit | *le* vieillard vers ce*tte*
con*jonc*tion s*u*prême ave*c la* probabi*lité* (n : ɔ̃)

Fiançailles: dont | *le* voile d'illus*i*on rej*ailli* leur
ha*n*tise | ain*s*i que le *fan*tôme d'un ge*s*te (ɑ : a)

immobilise: au ve*l*ours ch*iff*onné par un e*scla*ffe*m*ent
*s*om*b*re (z : s)

l'héroïque: *irré*sist*ib*le mais *con*tenu (ɔ : ɔ̃)

*rythmique suspens du sinistre: s'ens*evel*ir* / aux écu*m*es
    origi*n*elles / *n*aguères *d'*où *sur*saut*a s*on *d*élire
    j*usqu'*à *un*e *cim*e (p : d)

que le lieu: inf*é*r*ieu*r *c*l*a*potis *qu*el*con*q*u*e *c*omme pour
    disperser *l'ac*te vide (ø : œ)

When the phonetic substance of a word or phrase is scattered in this way through the syntactic sequence a strong counter-syntactic pressure is created. The later part of a sentence appears not simply to continue and develop the earlier part, but to provide it with a static reflection of itself. And this phonetic kinship invites the reader, as I have already remarked on a number of occasions, to perceive equivalence as well as sequence within the sentence, and to pursue semantic kinship between phrases that grammar requires to remain disparate. The phrases which contain the anagrams yield two messages: the relationship between the key-word and those which follow it, is at the same time the relationship between interdependent parts of a sentence and that between a word and its gloss, or a text and its commentary.

At these moments, we are in the realm of phantom definitions that so fascinated Michel Leiris in his *Glossaire j'y serre mes gloses* and *Biffures*.[21] Leiris's mind is sensitive – at times painfully and self-destructively sensitive – to the gap between word and thing, and seeks to reduce the arbitrariness of the verbal sign by means of spontaneous, phonetically inspired fantasy. Leiris is a 'cratylist'[22] of uncommon dexterity and inventive power, for whom many words appear to murmur their own definitions:

> AZUR – pur de toute bavure, une embrasure.
> MÉTAPHORE – phare de phosphore? forêt
> matée? ou épitaphe du fort en thème?
> MONADE – monde abrégé, nomade.
> TRANSCENDANCE – transe sans danse.[23]

Although Mallarmé's word-play is much more muted than this, similar effects are to be heard in counterpoint to the propositional senses of the poem: *puérile* is marginally redefined and remotivated by 'caressée et polie et rendue et lavée', as is *flétrie* by 'par la neutralité identique du gouffre' and *nul* by 'n'aura eu lieu'. Words blend into their verbal surroundings. Sense takes devious paths. The poem rewrites itself. But this movement is not simply one of increasing semantic dispersal. For Mallarmé's decisive formulae, despite the ironic reservations with which the text at large surrounds them, do much to reunify these divergent undercurrents. And the anagrammatical process itself may suggest closure and completeness of sense as well as indefinite ramification. At the end of the poem, for example, the sounds of the last line have appeared, with one exception [œ̃], in the six preceding phrases: 'veillant [eã] doutant [dutã] roulant [uã] brillant et méditant [ãemedtã] avant de s'arrêter [ãdsete] à quelque point dernier qui le sacre [kɛk(ə)pdɛeksk(ə)] Toute Pensée émet un Coup de Dés [tut pãse emɛ œ̃ ku d(ə) de]'. In this case the effect is a pronounced one of convergence and rediscovered cogency: the final line pulls the variegated sound materials of the earlier phrases into a sudden concentrated pattern. Here, as in all these cases of suggestive sound figuration, the meaning of the words is of supreme importance. It is clear that if Mallarmé's criteria in choosing a forcible last line had been purely phonetic ones, other sentences would have served as well: 'Tout comprendre c'est tout pardonner', for example, would have been an appealing candidate (whereas 'Dieu fait bien ce qu'il fait' would have had little to recommend it). These sound-induced submeanings of the text are one among many incitements to plural thinking offered by *Un Coup de dés*. No message in the poem, they remind us, is perfectly self-bounded and self-vindicating; each of them refers us elsewhere for the scale against which its implications are to be measured. Any portion of text is modifiable or refutable by any other portion, or by itself differently understood.

The second feature I shall mention is 'overdetermined' syntax. Many words and phrases belong to two or more syntactic sequences at once. The most arresting of these duplications are those which involve the title-sentence. For they allow that sentence to be read in two distinct perspectives – as flatly super-imposed upon the rest of the text, or as generated from within it, detail by detail. On (5), for instance, 'n'abolira' belongs to the predicate of the initial 'Un Coup de dés', and at the same time continues the sequence of verbs in the future tense which have 'le voile d'illusion' as their subject. (The latter relation-ship is reinforced by the sound-play *-lera -lera -oli- -olira.*) For one sinister moment the dice-throw and the inner hesitations and frailties which it seeks to overcome are revealed as synonymous and interchangeable; the argument of the poem has been cut short and the redeeming act prematurely dissolved within its own contrary. Similarly on (9) 'le hasard' completes the title-sentence and at the same time completes the conditional pro-position 'si c'était le nombre ce serait le hasard'. (The contrast between number and chance is strengthened on this page, and made visible at a glance, by typographical means.[24]) Chance is again doubly victorious. In both these cases the subsidiary sentence which is grafted upon the main one adds not a counter-suggestion but supporting evidence from a different source. Negation becomes an enveloping atmosphere. It is only by registering the differences of kind and intensity which exist between the writer's manifold, interwoven negatives that positive value may be discovered or adduced.

In examining the imagery of the poem one often finds a similar pattern of overdetermination. The following passage, for example, describes the return of the self to the realm of primitive undifferentiation within which its first, frail aspiration towards structure had come about:

> Choit / la plume / rythmique suspens du sinistre /
> s'ensevelir / aux écumes originelles / naguères d'où
> sursauta son délire jusqu'à une cime / flétrie / par
> la neutralité identique du gouffre (9)

But the self as it falls back is returning not to a chaos external to its sphere of action but to a turmoil from which it had never been perfectly free and which was reflected in its own internal

process. Its original upwards impulse had been delusive, a
heady and disordered pursuit of unreality ('d'où sursauta son
délire'), and its goal of splendid apartness had been vitiated
in advance; 'flétrie' is not a displaced epithet of the sort we find
in Keats's 'the two brothers and their murder'd man',[25] but a
piece of literal sense: at the moment when the aspiration is
launched it has already failed. Mallarmé here records the certain
failure of an uncertain escape towards an impossible goal.

The same idea as recast on the following page has an even
broader negative reach:

> inférieur clapotis quelconque comme pour disperser
> l'acte vide / abruptement qui sinon / par son
> mensonge / eût fondé / la perdition

The act which is annulled by shabby circumstance not only
would have failed anyway by virtue of the falsehood it promotes, but is *eo ipso* void. The act fails, that is to say, under
three heads – by being opposed from without, by being contaminated from within and by having vacancy and vanity as its
defining characteristics. But in neither of the passages I have
quoted does the repetition and 'overdetermination' of failure
create an impression of redundancy. For the human instincts
and activities referred to are manifold, and the syntax of both
passages is so delicately segmented that even in these plain
facts of despair and intellectual collapse positive energies
remain palpable. Loss is perceived in too many related ways at
once for the fact of loss to be merely brutal and incontrovertible.
Even here, even in the perception of debased and deadening
uniformity, a sense of the multiple potentialities of human
awareness has been preserved.

These, then, are a few of the ways in which Mallarmé's
exhaustive account of catastrophe in *Un Coup de dés* – of pattern
unperceived, sense ungrasped and hope unsustained – remains
emotionally and intellectually complex. The promise of pattern
is not present merely as an imprecise eleventh-hour expectation
('excepté à l'altitude peut-être une constellation'): it is immanent to the whole work. Every fragment is a momentary nucleus

of relationships which invite us to a positive, thoughtful collaboration with the text. Sound patterns by turns confirm and contest, disperse and crystallise, the propositions of the poem. The syntax binds divergent messages together and threads one negation into another with such exactitude that a new, perilous sense of positive value is created. The images present not single states of affairs or single tendencies of mind, but a dynamic series of intersecting events. All this compels the reader to think *between*, to measure distances, to make structures and break them, and, in response to the multiplicity of the text, to become multiple himself. In *Un Coup de dés* Mallarmé explores the *terra incognita* between negation and knowledge.

VI

Un Coup de dés is a complex picture of contingency and risk, and of those activities of will by which humans seek to discover pattern and purpose within their experience. The subject of the poem is simple and general. Mallarmé's 'hasard' is a condition of mind – the abidingly unstable medium of thought – and a condition also of the physical universe; the vulnerable and inventive self which is seen at work in the world – organising, controlling, game-playing, living against the odds, failing and starting again – is the human being at large. Although there are many touches of Romantic individualism in the working out of the main motifs – the captain ('prince amer de l'écueil') is a defiant moral solitary who takes pride in the singular anguish which his task imposes upon him – this whole imagery contributes to a portrait on the largest scale of a general human predicament: indeed, the scale of the portrait, if not its tone, would have been readily understood by Hume or Voltaire. Mallarmé's vision of a universally accidental world is far too grandly conceived for mere idiosyncrasies of character and emotional disposition to play more than a supporting part. What matters in the poem is the necessarily adverse conditions in which creative human gestures take place, and the special capacities of mind and heart by which human beings are equipped for this unequal contest.

I have already touched upon a number of the problems which these issues raise for the poet. The most important of them is that of realising a poetic structure which will allow chance its weight and its omnipresence while allowing the fragile ordering impulse of the human being its proper dialectical edge. The poem could so easily have lapsed from the tension and the comprehensiveness of this theme. If one narrow margin had been overstepped *Un Coup de dés* would have been no more than chaos triumphant; if another had been overstepped, it would have been no more than an unfamiliar view of a familiar subject: domestic man safely surveying the tumults which begin on the far side of his threshold. Mallarmé has solved the problem with remarkable ingenuity by representing his chaos not as nonsense but as the realm of indefinitely multiple and replenishable significance, and creating for his 'hero' the role of a beleaguered pattern-seeker. And a fine balance is kept as the contest unfolds. The worst that can happen and the best that can happen are not equally possible and mutually exclusive futures: they are twin versions of the present moment, twin ways of seeing and inhabiting the world. Every moment is the complete wager.

The plural suggestiveness of Mallarmé's textures in *Un Coup de dés* provides an apt dramatic context for his epistemological enquiries. The meanings one cannot quite seize, the multitude of teasing ideas which appear *en profil perdu*, create a rich associative field within which achieved ideas matter. The main lesson of the text, as it re-teaches us to read, is that we must be prepared to pursue its latent dispositions as well as its declared themes. Many kinds of approximate, speculative thinking are required of us if we are to understand the poem fully at its moments of promptness and precision. We must be prepared to take seriously events occurring on the edges of consciousness, and allow pattern to emerge gradually and indirectly ('selon telle obliquité par telle declivité').

Maurice Blanchot, in his admirable essay on the poem in *Le Livre à venir*, has written in these terms about the multidimensional language within which our scannings take place:

Cette langue nouvelle que l'on prétend que
Mallarmé s'est créée par on ne sait quel désir
d'ésotérisme [...] est une langue stricte, destinée à
élaborer, selon des voies nouvelles, l'espace propre
au langage, que nous autres, dans la prose
quotidienne comme dans l'usage littéraire, nous
réduisons à une simple surface parcourue par un
mouvement uniforme et irréversible. A cet espace,
Mallarmé restitue la profondeur. Une phrase ne se
contente pas de se dérouler d'une manière linéaire ;
elle s'ouvre ; par cette ouverture s'étagent, se
dégagent, s'espacent et se resserrent, à des
profondeurs de niveaux différents, d'autres
mouvements de phrases, d'autres rythmes de
paroles, qui sont en rapport les uns avec
les autres selon de fermes déterminations de
structure, quoique étrangères à la logique ordinaire
– logique de subordination – laquelle détruit
l'espace et uniformise le mouvement.[26]

And Blanchot characterises with particular insight the underlying rhythms of dispersal and convergence which punctuate
this complex linguistic space.[27]

The extraordinary thing about this space is its sheer power of
inclusion: it is non-linear, yet contains powerful linearities
within it; it invites us to depart from the syntactic mode of
organisation, yet is founded upon a close knowledge and
observance of French syntax; it is a self-bounding linguistic
universe, yet at the same time a working model of mental
process. If our first impression on picking up Mallarmé's book
is that the poet in writing it was somehow interested in the
expressive power of *empty* space, the experience of reading the
text rapidly suggests otherwise. The space created by the poem
is for Mallarmé no more empty than physical space is for
Descartes or for Einstein.[28] It is rather a 'field', a comprehensive realm of interrelated energies, which are organised yet
indefinitely subject to mutation and inflection.

But precisely the 'field' character of *Un Coup de dés* raises a problem. Throughout my discussion I have been assuming more or less tacitly that the reader's mind, placing itself within the field of the text, will consent to cooperate optimistically and creatively with that text, and will enjoy becoming increasingly aware of itself as a multi-dimensional manifold. Yet how differently *Un Coup de dés* may act upon us at certain moments. It can by the very richness of its spatialised, self-anagrammatising and self-rewriting textures suggest that the human being, for all his mighty aspirations towards order, is no more than a detail – a local inflection of the field – and that none of his gestures can ever change anything. Like so many of the external 'perspectives' which one may be tempted to adopt in order to shape one's experience of the poem, this notion has been written into it by Mallarmé with magnificent simplicity: 'rien n'aura eu lieu que le lieu'. This sense of human smallness and helplessness is only part of the world that *Un Coup de dés* creates for us, just as the statement I have quoted is only part of the culmination of the poem. But it is a further lesson of the text that parts can at any moment, and whether or not we wish them to, become encompassing wholes.

Concluding Note

... fie upon 'But yet'!
'But yet' is as a gaoler to bring forth
Some monstrous malefactor.
SHAKESPEARE: *Antony and Cleopatra*

But yet, when the virtues of a difficult art have fully impressed themselves upon us, when a discourse that is all zig-zags, contrapuntal contrivances and variously encoded states of doubt has come at last to seem the model of honest human utterance, how glorious it may still be to hear other, plainer artists speak out loud and bold. Suddenly, remembering the struggles and despairs that the extraction of sense from difficult poems has caused us, we may find that simplicity of statement has acquired a new prestige in our eyes. The artist who makes important statements singly, clearly and economically may present himself to the weary intelligence as the true hero of letters. Besides, many readers of literature will have an instinctive respect for clear statements properly framed and concatenated, and will admire them the more when the matters in question are complex and could as easily have issued in confusion. Lionel Trilling has reminded us that intellectual cogency may have its own aesthetic power; he gives Yeats's couplet:

> We had fed the heart on fantasies,
> The heart's grown brutal from the fare.

and Freud's last book *An Outline of Psychoanalysis* as formulations which were to him cogent in this way. They gave 'the pleasure of listening to a strong, decisive, self-limiting voice uttering statements to which I can give assent.'[1] The fact that Mallarmé does not often afford us this pleasure, and that we may find ourselves assenting to certain of his works only after much perplexity and hesitation, is, it seems to me, a genuine cause for concern.

The trouble is not just that Mallarmé does not 'say' what he 'means' and that in not doing so he risks being seriously misunderstood; difficulty itself can sometimes appear as a gratuitous cult of indirectness, a box of tricks, a fad. In arguing the case for Mallarmé's difficulty as legitimate and productive, I started from certain of his central achievements – poems in which, I suggested, the conceptual and existential problems at issue were of a complexity sufficient to justify and at the same time to control their involved and indefinitely reconstruable verbal textures. The whole question of difficulty would have looked different if I had concentrated upon his *vers de circonstance* or others of his lesser works. For Mallarmé, as is well known, had among many talents those of the genteel versifier and the maker of coyly allusive bagatelles. Difficulty might easily have emerged in the course of such a discussion as an art of teasing, a dispensable elegance, which Mallarmé simply failed to relinquish when his themes and purposes became more substantial. But while it is clear to me that such a view of 'Prose' or *Un Coup de dés* would be false, the charge that the difficulty of these poems is thinly motivated cannot be shrugged off. An important and stubborn doubt may underlie the charge.

Poems which are as difficult and broken in texture as these, and which invite the reader to perform so many alternative kinds of scansion, may seem to be founded upon a disconcerting invisible premise: that what matters in opinions, beliefs, tenets and convictions, and in the axioms, propositions, apophthegms or figurative expressions in which such inward dispositions are made public, is not their capacity to answer questions about the world, but their capacity to provoke doubt and to become the objects of doubt. Such a suspicion cannot of course be finally confirmed or dispelled by a patient reading of the text. But this does not mean that we are entitled to disregard it. For if the reader begins to suspect that Mallarmé's indirectness is the product of an unexamined predilection for ideas in their mutant or deviant forms, or that Mallarmé declines for reasons of mere intellectual delicacy to utter upon matters that are self-evidently or demonstrably the case, the difficulty of the poems is likely to appear sham and irresponsible. Seen in that light the assumption upon which the poems are built may appear to be not the strong one that I proposed at the end of my second chapter – that the pursuit of knowledge is necessarily chequered, mobile and nourished by discontinuity – but the extremely weak one that plain statements even where they are right may easily be dull, and should therefore be avoided by those seeking to display largeness and subtlety of mind. Difficulty, it must be granted, *may* originate in a simple refusal to see the obvious and to come clean about it.

But what kinds of doubt are these? Are they of the kind that one might raise about the music of Schoenberg's atonal period when considering it from the viewpoint of diatonic harmony, or about the polysemantic fabric of *Finnegans Wake* from the viewpoint of the nineteenth-century mimetic novel, or about Bridget Riley's pictorial space from the viewpoint of Gainsborough's? Are we, that is to say, in wondering thus about the premises of Mallarmé's poetic act, just asking one of those questions which major cultural schisms notoriously compel us to ask but which are seldom to be answered in terms which both parties would find coherent? My answer to this is a qualified 'yes'. Mallarmé in these late poems takes us into a world where negative states and statements have an informing role in artistic creation, and a world which twentieth-century art has continued tenaciously to explore. The question 'are Mallarmé's powers of doubt, refusal and conceptual mutation responsibly used?' is one local variant of a question that whole areas of modern art invite its admirers to ask, and that much so-called 'minimal', 'poor' or 'aleatory' art facilely scandalises its audiences with.

The new poetry which Mallarmé has created is one in which shunning eloquence, flattening the hierarchies of discourse and refusing to be predicative or consequential may be integral parts of the artistic endeavour; and this poetry may be profoundly disturbing to those who value works of art as a means of limiting plurality, controlling contradiction and rediscovering

continuities within the world and the self. Earlier in this study
I showed that Mallarmé's negative response to the demands of
conventional linear discourse plays a crucial part in making his
texts into 'open' or 'pluralised' semantic systems, and that he
presupposes in us a considerable tolerance for uncertainty.
But these poems are disturbing not simply because they produce
and interfuse many meanings at once but because they thereby
make the reader an accomplice in the business of negation.
They are so resolutely overdetermined, so much in surplus
semantically, that they impose upon the reader who wishes to
read whole poems rather than fragments the task of censoring
and excluding sense. We recoil from the dangerous sphere of
total information into which Mallarmé seems at moments to be
summoning us, but in doing so we assume an uncommon
burden of responsibility. For the distinction between mattering
supremely and mattering not at all has not been established by
the artist within the text: it is ours to make, and may be gained
or lost in a blink. These are the elements of a new aesthetic
which Mallarmé did much to pioneer and which are incommensurate with those upon which earlier nineteenth-century
poetry was founded.

But my 'yes' is qualified because the whole story is not being
told if we tackle the question like this, and one of Mallarmé's
main claims to authenticity is being silenced. If we say that
Mallarmé's use of 'negativity' in his poetry is not sham and
irresponsible because 'negativity' is at the heart of the modern
poem, being the very means by which its multiplicity is guaran-
teed, we are likely to misrepresent his scrupulous and terrible
account of death as the ultimate negation. If we present negations as simply immanent to the poetic text – as 'the way these
poems work' – death may appear as tame and undramatic, or
may quite dissolve from sight into mere omnipresence.

Mallarmé writes about death with unmatched intensity, but its
role in the poems is not easy to characterise. For although death
is not just immanent to them, neither is it a detachable theme,
issue or debating point. Rather it arises urgently within the
plural poetic texture as an uncrossable limitation placed upon

meaning, or as an arbitrary cessation of meaning against which there is no appeal. This texture has been my main preoccupation in the foregoing pages. I have spoken about the ways in which assertions and negations, arguments and counter-arguments, are woven together syntactically, and about the ways in which the syntax of the poems is diffracted by the other prominent systems – metrical, phonetic or 'spatial' – which adjoin it. I have spoken about the sense of plenitude which Mallarmé's poems create for us, and about the special role which the speculative intelligence of the reader comes to play in organising the multiple potentialities of the text. This, I have suggested, is the volatile and self-replenishing context without which Mallarmé's metaphysical enquiries could easily have seemed inert and stale. And this is where death enters, into this full world where eye and ear and rhythmic sense and image-and-concept-handling intelligence are all together engaged and energised. A single phrase may appear to bear the whole expressive weight:

> . . .l'horreur du sol où le plumage est pris

> Avant qu'un sépulcre ne rie

> la neutralité identique du gouffre

But these phrases are perfectly prepared for within the text: what is being threatened in them is not only a various life lived beyond the confines of the poem, but the poetic process itself. The destruction of sense which is essential to the maintenance of the textual manifold is suddenly seen not as a creative instrument but as the tracing within the text of an irreversible human destiny. At these moments a whole realm of foreboding and risk which the poems explore reaches its point of cruellest immediacy. In the pursuit of sense, sense is irrecoverably lost.

I am conscious, when suggesting that Mallarmé has the power to hurt, that I am in breach of much that is considered proper in modern criticism. So many of our current critical notions – I am thinking, for example, of 'aesthetic distance', 'organic form', the 'intentional fallacy' and the 'fingernail-paring artist removed from his work', to say nothing of that 'disappearance of the subject' which has won so many easy victories in recent French thought – encourage us to play safe, to be defensive or complacent and to keep the cutting edges of works of art discreetly from view. If we begin our critical explorations with the chaste assumption that works of art are 'well-wrought urns', that they are self-bounded worlds in which all tensions are internally resolved and all pains internally soothed and that the personality of their creator (if he has a personality) is irrelevant to them, we shall of course find exactly these things to be the case. But our experience as readers, spectators or listeners may be completely different; we may be moved by works of art in ways that our official critical procedures make no allowance for: we may be haunted by a single chromaticism in a Mozart quintet, or by the slant of a fierce, disconsolate eye in one of the later self-portraits of Rembrandt. Something is going wrong when criticism conscientiously refuses to take heed of the singular disruptive energies which works of art possess, and quite as badly wrong when those energies are normalised by being made into a test of political acceptability. I am not suggesting that Mallarmé is an artist in terror, a manipulator of our fears, but that his poems do at moments make rapid thrusts against the reader's sense of his own coherence, and that in Mallarmé's account the negative in human experience can be complete and irremoveable. This is the sort of thing that analysis can do little to preserve or to imitate, but that has too intimate a place in these works to be left unspoken in criticism.

The classic human answers to death – the myths, creeds, systems, logics in which our alleviation lies – are all present in Mallarmé's work: the swan may fly, the poem may be written, the supreme flower may be shown forth, the constellation may appear in the night sky. But in Mallarmé's case how transparently portrayed and unsuperstitious these answers are and how much less important, finally, is what they propose than the inveterately human power which seeks to check or replace them – the power which enables Mallarmé in the face of terror, as in the face of joy, to pronounce his slender, strong 'but yet'.

APPENDIX

The earlier version of 'Prose pour des Esseintes' (without title)[1]

Indéfinissable, ô Mémoire,
Par ce midi, ne rêves-tu
L'Hyperbole, aujourd'hui grimoire
Dans un livre de fer vêtu?

Car j'installe par la Science
L'hymne des cœurs spirituels
En l'œuvre de ma patience,
Atlas, herbiers et rituels.

Nous promenions notre visage –
Nous fûmes deux! je le maintiens,
Sur maints charmes de paysage
Aurais-je su dire: les siens!

L'ère d'infinité se trouble
Lorsque, sans nul motif, on dit
De ce climat que notre double
Inconscience approfondit,

Que, sol des cent iris, son site,
Ils savent s'il a, certe, été,
Ne porte pas de nom que cite
Entre tous ses fastes, l'Eté.

Oui, dans une île que l'air charge
De vue et non de visions,
Toute fleur s'étalait plus large
Sans que nous en devisions.

Telles, immenses, que chacune
Ordinairement se para
D'un lucide contour, lacune
Qui du jour pur la sépara.

Obsession! Désir, idées,
Tout en moi triomphait de voir
La famille des iridées
Connaître le nouveau devoir,

Mais cette sœur, sensée et tendre,
Ne porta ses regards plus loin
Que moi-même: et tels, les lui rendre
Devenait mon unique soin.

Oh! sache l'Esprit de litige,
A cette heure où nous nous taisons,
Que de multiples lis la tige
Grandissait trop pour nos raisons,

Et non, comme en pleure la rive! –
Car le jeu monotone ment
Pour qui l'ampleur de l'île arrive
Seul, en mon jeune étonnement

D'entendre le Ciel et la carte
Sans fin attestés sur nos pas
Par l'onde même qui s'écarte,
Que ce pays n'exista pas!

Ce fut de la finale extase
Le sens, quand, grave et par chemin,
Elle dit ce terme: Anasthase! –
Gravé sur quelque parchemin,

Avant qu'un sépulchre ne rie
Sous aucun climat, son aïeul,
De porter ce nom: Pulchérie! –
Caché par le trop grand glaïeul.

NOTES

Unless otherwise stated, place of publication for works
mentioned below is Paris for books in French and London
for those in English.

PREFATORY NOTE

1 It should not be forgotten that certain powerful commentators have seen Mallarmé's verse as a sign of the degeneration
of modern literary culture; Mallarmé figures as villain in such
polemical works as Max Nordau's *Entartung* (1892) and
Zeitgenössische Franzosen (1901), Tolstoy's *What is Art?* (1898)
and Julien Benda's *La France byzantine* (1945).

2 'Obscurity in Poetry', *Collected Essays in Literary Criticism*,
Second Edition, Faber and Faber, 1951, 100. Maurice
Blanchot has repudiated in the following terms the notion
that Mallarmé's work is obscure: 'Il est même à croire que
son œuvre ne pouvait lui apparaître que pure de toute
énigme, sans le voile de la plus légère obscurité, car énigme et
obscurité lui auraient fait supposer qu'on entrait dans ses
poèmes sans cesser de rester au-dehors, qu'on les regardait
d'un point de vue non poétique, qu'on les confrontait, dans
une intention de défi ou d'enseignement, avec les moyens de
la raison discursive, attitude qui n'était pas illégitime en
elle-même mais qui ne pouvait que rester étrangère au poète
et lui sembler inconcevable. L'accusation d'obscurité que la
critique n'a cessé de porter contre lui, n'a donc de sens que
pour l'intelligence non poétique, ou plus exactement que si
l'on imagine, par une hypothèse singulière, que l'œuvre de
Mallarmé n'appartient pas à la poésie. On est alors libre de la
juger énigmatique et même de l'expliquer, de la séparer de ses
énigmes, de même qu'on est toujours libre de donner un
commentaire littéraire d'une œuvre musicale, de l'interpréter
comme un symbole des luttes propres de l'esprit.' ('La
Poésie de Mallarmé est-elle obscure?', *Faux pas*, Gallimard,
1943, 130.) Jean Cohen argues in his elliptic 'L'"Obscurité"
de Mallarmé' (*Revue d'esthétique*, t.15, fasc.1, jan.–mars 1962,
64–72) that the problem of obscurity is essentially a formal/
structural one and that the content-based exegetical tradition
has seriously misrepresented it.

CHAPTER ONE

1 The intellectual complexity of the poetry of this period has been studied with rare insight by Odette de Mourgues in her *Metaphysical, Baroque and Précieux Poetry*, Oxford, Clarendon Press, 1953. She writes: 'Fulke Greville, like Scève, is a difficult poet. He may have had personal reasons for being deliberately obscure. But we are struck, when reading his poems and tragedies, by a sort of natural passion for making the most of his intellectual powers and exacting the same effort from the reader...' (23).

2 The term 'paradigm' in the sense of 'dominant scientific orthodoxy' was launched by Thomas S. Kuhn, in *The Structure of Scientific Revolutions,* University of Chicago Press, 1962. He writes that, in choosing the term, he meant 'to suggest that some accepted examples of actual scientific practice – examples which include law, theory, application, and instrumentation together – provide models from which spring particular coherent traditions of scientific research.' (Second Edition, 1970, 10.)

3 *Œuvres complètes,* ed. Henri Mondor and G. Jean-Aubry, 'Bibliothèque de la Pléiade', Gallimard, 1951, 50. In all subsequent references to this edition the initials *O.c.* will be used.

4 The whole poem is printed on pp. 21–3 of the present volume. References to individual lines of the poem will be given throughout in the form: quatrain number plus line number (6.3, 14.2 and so forth).

5 *O.c.,* 67.

6 *O.c.,* 68.

7 *O.c.,* 71.

8 The third of these possibilities is the one favoured by Gardner Davies in his valuable analysis of the sonnet (*Les 'Tombeaux' de Mallarmé,* Corti, 1950, 131–63). The first impact upon the reader of a comparably ambiguous line ('Hilare or de cymbale à des poings irrité') is vividly described by L. J. Austin in his 'Mallarmé's Reshaping of "Le Pitre châtié" ', *Order and Adventure in Post-Romantic French Poetry. Essays presented to C. A. Hackett,* ed. E. M. Beaumont, J. M. Cocking and J. Cruickshank, Oxford, Blackwell, 1973, 62.

9 On the perils of the real/ideal dichotomy as applied to Mallarmé, see L. J. Austin, 'Mallarmé et le réel', *Modern Miscellany* (presented to Eugène Vinaver), ed. T. E. Lawrenson, F. E. Sutcliffe, G. F. A. Gadoffre, Manchester, The University Press, 1969, 12-24. For two sharply contrasting views of Mallarmé's handling and dissolution of this dichotomy, see Albert Béguin, *L'Ame romantique et le rêve,* nouvelle édition, Corti, 1946, 381–3 and Yves Bonnefoy, *L'Improbable,* Mercure de France, 1959, 152–5.

10 *O.c.*, 67–8. In the Pléiade *Œuvres complètes* 'infligée' (line 10) is misprinted as 'infligé'. Commentaries on this sonnet are to be found in most of the general works on Mallarmé mentioned in subsequent footnotes. On the sound-patterning, see Elizabeth Sewell, *The Structure of Poetry*, Routledge and Kegan Paul, 1951, 144–6; on the 'intuitive and instinctive' logic of Mallarmé's imagery, and the relations between this sonnet and 'Prose', see A. R. Chisholm, 'Mallarmé: *"Le vierge, le vivace..."*', *French Studies*, Vol. XVI, No. 4, October 1962, 359–63; on the polyvalence of this sonnet and its 'concurrence of contexts', see Robert Champigny, 'The *Swan* and the Question of Pure Poetry', *L'Esprit Créateur*, Vol. 1, No. 3, Fall 1961, 145–55. On Mallarmé as sonneteer, see David H. T. Scott, *Sonnet Theory and Practice in Nineteenth-Century France: Sonnets on the Sonnet*, Occasional Papers in Modern Languages, No. 12, Hull, University of Hull Publications, 1977.

11 For a fuller account of these lines, see below pp. 34, 36, 44–6. The phrase 'L'ère d'autorité' offers one of the most interesting points of comparison with the early version of 'Prose' (see Appendix pp. 155–6) where 'L'ère d'infinité' occurs instead. But what does the variant tell us about the meaning of the phrase? We cannot know, simply from the inspection of two portions of text (however extensively that inspection is supported by knowledge of Mallarmé's general habits of thought and composition), whether the poet was motivated in making his change by a desire to say more or less the same thing but in more appropriate/felicitous/logical words, or by a desire to bring a new range of meaning into play. My own guess, in the present case, would be that 'infinité' was removed because it gave an odd and unsatisfactory circularity to the sentence. The era of infinity is disturbed by that infinity which (we may assume) resides in the non-terrestrial flowers. Infinity in the new version is quite properly made to disturb something other than itself (*autorité* suggesting, say, the cult of clear rational explanation). On change (as distinct from heightening) of meaning between variants, see Alison Fairlie, ' "Mène-t-on la foule dans les ateliers?" – Some Remarks on Baudelaire's Variants', *Order and Adventure* (see Note 8 above), 18–19.

12 Weidenfeld and Nicolson, 1967.

13 See in particular Chapters Five and Six, 64–94.

CHAPTER TWO

1 *A la recherche du temps perdu*, ed. Pierre Clarac and André Ferré, Vol. 2, 'Bibliothèque de la Pléiade', Gallimard, 1954, 51.

2 *Œuvres*, ed. Jean Hytier, Vol. 1, 'Bibliothèque de la Pléiade', Gallimard, 1957, 1356.

3 See *Poetics*, 1449B–1450A (appearing on pp. 34–9 of Ingram Bywater's translation, Oxford, Clarendon Press, 1920).

4 *The Rambler*, No. 94, is devoted to the question of sound and sense in verse. Johnson writes: 'It is scarcely to be doubted, that on many occasions we make the musick which we imagine ourselves to hear; that we modulate the poem by our own disposition, and ascribe to the numbers the effects of the sense.' (*Works*, Vol. IV, ed. W. J. Bate and Albrecht B. Strauss, Yale University Press, 1969, 136). In the same essay, Johnson gives many examples in which numbers *do* reinforce the effects of the sense. The error with which he is concerned is that of assuming that a particular phonetic feature, being expressive in one context, would have a similar expressive value in others where the sense is different or in direct conflict.

5 This work first appeared in 1904. I shall refer to the third (revised) edition, Champion, 1923.

6 Thibaudet, for example, writes as follows about the rhymes of 'Le vierge, le vivace...': 'Elles développent sur la voyelle aiguë et contractée la monotonie d'un vaste espace solitaire, silencieux, tout blanc de glace dure.' Later in the same paragraph he notes, astonishingly: 'Le dernier vers des quatrains étale d'un grand geste nu, sous le soleil froid qui l'éclaire, la congélation qu'il exprime.' (*La Poésie de Stéphane Mallarmé*, Gallimard, 1926, 250.) For a strongly worded statement on subjectivism dressed up as science in the analysis of verse, see Archibald A. Hill (reviewing works by Pierre Guiraud and Herbert Seidler) in *Language*, Vol. 31, No. 2, April–June 1955, 249–52.

7 *The Great Chain of Being*, New York, Harper and Row, 1960, 25. For the classic Platonic statement of the 'otherworldly' theme, see *Phaedo* 84A–B.

8 Ibid., 26.

9 We should not forget that 'Prose' is the product of one phase in Mallarmé's creative life, and the culmination of one strain within his thinking. Earlier he had formulated his fundamental metaphysical questions quite differently. In a celebrated letter of April 1866 to Henri Cazalis, for example, he wrote: 'Oui, *je le sais*, nous ne sommes que de vaines formes de la matière, mais bien sublimes pour avoir inventé Dieu et notre âme. Si sublimes, mon ami! que je veux me donner ce spectacle de la matière, ayant conscience d'être et, cependant, s'élançant forcenément dans le Rêve qu'elle sait n'être pas, chantant l'Ame et toutes les divines impressions pareilles qui se sont amassées en nous depuis les premiers âges et proclament, devant le Rien qui est la vérité, ces glorieux mensonges! / Tel est le plan de mon volume lyrique et tel sera peut-être son titre, *La Gloire du mensonge*, ou *Le Glorieux Mensonge*. Je chanterai en désespéré!' (*Correspondance*,

Vol. I, 1862–1871, ed. Henri Mondor and Jean-Pierre
Richard, Gallimard, 1959, 207–8). It would be possible –
though in my view unproductive – to see Mallarmé's
presentation of the Ideas in 'Prose' as a quest for a supreme
redemptive fiction of this kind. On the affinities between
Mallarmé and Plato, see Guy Delfel, *L'Esthétique de Stéphane
Mallarmé*, Flammarion, 1951, Robert Champigny,
'Mallarmé's Relation to Platonism and Romanticism', *The
Modern Language Review*, Vol. LI, No. 3, July 1956, 348–58,
and Gérard Genette, *Mimologiques*, Seuil, 1976 (see Note 113).

10 See especially 595, 598–607. This is Plato's view not of *all*
artists, but of representative (or 'imitative') artists in
particular. Certain non-representative poets are allowed to
remain in the city (607A). Elsewhere in the Platonic corpus
(e.g. *Phaedrus* 245A, *Meno* 81A–C) a more favourable view of
poets is expressed. For a strongly argued rejection of the
popular notion of a Platonic 'attack on art', see R. G.
Collingwood, *The Principles of Art*, Oxford, Clarendon
Press, 1938, 46–52, 97–100. E. R. Dodds writes of Plato in
The Greeks and the Irrational, Berkeley and Los Angeles,
University of California Press, 1951, that 'while he [. . .]
accepted (with whatever ironical reservations) the poet, the
prophet, and the "corybantic" as being in some sense
channels of divine or daemonic grace, he nevertheless rated
their activities far below those of the rational self, and held
that they must be subject to the control and criticism of
reason, since reason was for him no passive plaything of
hidden forces, but an active manifestation of deity in man, a
daemon in its own right.' (218) See also Iris Murdoch's
brilliantly empathic *The Fire and the Sun*, Oxford, Clarendon
Press, 1977.

11 The three relevant tractates of *The Enneads* are I.6 on 'Beauty',
III.8 on 'Nature, Contemplation and the One' and V.8 'On
the Intellectual Beauty' (to be found in Stephen MacKenna's
translation (Fourth Edition, Faber and Faber, 1969) on pp.
56–64, 239–50 and 422–33). Erwin Panofsky contrasts the
Platonic and Plotinian views in the following terms: '. . . the
Platonic attack accuses the arts of continually arresting man's
inner vision within the realm of sensory images, that is, of
actually obstructing his contemplation of the world of Ideas;
and the Plotinian defense condemns the arts to the tragic fate
of eternally driving man's inner eye beyond these sensory
images, that is, of opening to him the prospect of the world
of Ideas but at the same time veiling the view. Understood as
copies of the sensory world, works of art are divested of a
more elevated spiritual or, if you will, symbolic meaning;
understood as revelations of Ideas, they are divested of the
timeless validity and self-sufficiency which properly belongs

to them. It seems that unless the theory of Ideas gives up its own metaphysical standpoint, it must perforce deny to the work of art either the one or the other.' (*Idea, a Concept in Art Theory*, trans. Joseph Peake, Columbia, University of South Carolina Press, 1968, 31–2. This useful short work appeared in its original German edition as *Idea. Ein Beitrag zur Begriffsgeschichte der älteren Kunsttheorie* (Studien der Bibliothek Warburg, 5), Leipzig–Berlin, 1924).

12 See below, pp. 78–83.

13 Notably Daniel Boulay, *L'Obscurité esthétique de Mallarmé et la 'Prose pour des Esseintes'*, chez l'auteur, 57 *bis.* av. de la Motte-Picquet, 1960, 27ff, and Olivier Dumas, 'Mallarmé, Platon et "La Prose pour des Esseintes"', *Revue des sciences humaines*, No. 126, avril–juin 1967, 239–57. Dumas records a number of allusions to, or chance coincidences with, Plato in Mallarmé's poem. Certain of these cases are interesting and instructive (he points, for example, to Socrates's myth of the 'upper earth', the dwelling-place of souls after death (*Phaedo* 109D–112E), as a possible model for Mallarmé's transcendent island in 'Prose'), while others are fanciful (he wonders whether 'ce midi' (4.3) might be an allusion to *Phaedrus* 242A in which Socrates is asked to wait until the noonday heat has abated before going on his way...).

14 The doctrine is explained in full, and relevant scholarship reviewed, by R. Hackforth in his *Plato's Phaedo* (translation, introduction and commentary), Cambridge University Press, 1955, 73–7. On the primitive origins of the doctrine, see Dodds, *The Greeks and the Irrational*, 209–10.

15 Georges Poulet, in his first general essay on Mallarmé (*La Distance Intérieure*, Plon, 1952, 298–355), writes as follows about the poet's idea of memory: 'A la différence de Proust, la mémoire chez Mallarmé n'est pas la reviviscence totale d'une impression primitive. Elle ne veut restituer ni les nuances de l'émotion, ni l'image particulière des objets qui la provoquèrent. C'est une mémoire notionnelle. Des objets remémorés elle laisse seulement "émaner, sans la gêne d'un proche ou concret rappel, la notion pure" (*O.c.*, 368). [...] L'éloignement temporel n'a donc pas eu seulement pour effet de reculer l'objet dans la perspective, il l'a détaché de toute actualité, même accomplie, de toute contingence, même passée...' (316–17).

16 See J. E. Raven, *Plato's Thought in the Making*, Cambridge University Press, 1965, 39–41.

17 *The Poetical Works*, ed. E. de Selincourt and Helen Darbishire, Vol. 4, Oxford, Clarendon Press, 1947, 281.

18 Evidence on Mallarmé's reading of philosophers is extremely scanty. Gabriel Faure tells us, for example, in his *Mallarmé à Tournon*, Éditions des Horizons de France, 1946: 'Rarement,

il monte jusqu'à la bibliothèque [du lycée], pourtant très riche
alors; c'est à peine si, en trois ans, il emprunte quelques
ouvrages de philosophie et quelques poètes de la Renais-
sance.' (42) But no source for this information is given, and
nothing further on the matter is said.

19 For a review of scholarly work on the relationship between
Mallarmé and Hegel, and an account of Mallarmé's possible
imaginative debt to Hegel in the years 1866–71, see Jean-
Pierre Richard, *L'Univers imaginaire de Mallarmé*, Seuil 1961,
231–3. See also L. J. Austin, 'Mallarmé et le rêve du "Livre"',
Mercure de France, t. CCCXVII, No. 1073, janvier 1953, 81–108,
and Gardner Davies, *Vers une explication rationnelle du 'Coup
de Dés'*, Corti, 1953, 33–52. On the need for caution in the
handling of this Hegelian influence see the comments by Carl
Barbier, Alan Raitt and Austin Gill in the proceedings of the
Colloque Mallarmé (Glasgow, novembre 1973) *en l'honneur de
Austin Gill*, ed. Carl P. Barbier, Nizet, 1975, 25–6.

20 *Correspondance*, Vol. I, 1862–1871, ed. Henri Mondor and
Jean-Pierre Richard, Gallimard, 1959, 249.

21 'Mallarmé, Huysmans et la "Prose pour des Esseintes"',
Revue d'Histoire Littéraire de la France, 54ᵉ année, No. 2, avril–
juin 1954, 145–83; 'Du nouveau sur la "Prose pour des
Esseintes" de Mallarmé', *Mercure de France*, t. CCCXXIII, No.
1097, jan.–avril 1955, 84–104; 'Mallarmé and the "Prose pour
des Esseintes"', *Forum for Modern Language Studies*, Vol. II,
No. 3, July 1966, 197–213. The third of these is by far the
most useful general introduction that we have to the poem.
For a broad view of the early scholarly achievement, see
Gardner Davies, 'Stéphane Mallarmé: Fifty Years of
Research', *French Studies*, Vol. I, No. 1, January 1947, 1–26.

22 In addition to the works mentioned in this paragraph, the
following are among the books and articles which have
appeared since Austin's original review and which are of
special interest for the study of 'Prose'.
BOOKS: Robert Goffin, *Mallarmé vivant*, Nizet, 1956; Léon
Cellier, *Mallarmé et la morte qui parle,* Presses Universitaires
de France, 1959; Henri Mondor, *Autres précisions sur Mallarmé
et Inédits*, Gallimard, 1961; Charles Chadwick, *Mallarmé. Sa
pensée dans sa poésie*, Corti, 1962; A. R. Chisholm, *Mallarmé's
'Grand Œuvre'*, Manchester, The University Press, 1962;
Robert Greer Cohn, *Toward the Poems of Mallarmé*, Berkeley
and Los Angeles, University of California Press, 1965;
É. Noulet, *Vingt poèmes de Stéphane Mallarmé. Exégèses*, 'Textes
littéraires français', Genève, Droz, 1967; D. J. Mossop,
*Pure Poetry. Studies in French Poetic Theory and Practice 1746 to
1945*, Oxford, Clarendon Press, 1971; Julia Kristeva, *La
Révolution du langage poétique*, Seuil, 1974; Simonne Verdin,
Stéphane Mallarmé, le presque contradictoire, précédé d'une

Étude de variantes, Nizet, 1975.

ARTICLES: Jacques Douchin, 'La "Prose pour des Esseintes" ou l'examen de conscience de Mallarmé', *Orbis Litterarum* (Copenhagen), t. XVII, fasc. 1–2, 1962, 82–99; D. J. Mossop, 'Mallarmé's "Prose pour des Esseintes"', *French Studies,* Vol. XVIII, No. 2, April 1964, 123–35; Olivier Dumas, 'Mallarmé, Platon et "La Prose pour des Esseintes"', *Revue des sciences humaines,* No. 126, avril–juin 1967, 239–57; Pierre-Olivier Walzer, 'Prolégomènes à toute exégèse future de la "Prose",' *Festgabe Hans von Greyerz, sum sechzigsten Geburtstag, 5. April 1967,* Bern, Herbert Lang, 1967, 809–15; Simonne Verdin, '"Prose pour des Esseintes". Exégèse', *Revue de l'Université de Bruxelles,* nouvelle série, 20ᵉ année, oct. 1967–jan. 1968, 122–46; Jacques Duchesne-Guillemin, 'Sur la "Prose"', *Synthèses,* 22ᵉ année, déc. 1967–jan. 1968, 57–60 (in the same issue, see also Robert Goffin's 'Rétrospections', 66–8 and Simonne Verdin's 'L'Action restreinte', 113–18); Eric Gans, 'Prose poétique', *Romanic Review,* Vol. LXVI, No. 3, May 1975, 187–98.

23 Chez l'auteur, 57 *bis.* av. de la Motte-Picquet, 1960.

24 Seuil, 1961, 400–3 and *passim.*

25 Plon, 1961, 431–53. See also *Entre moi et moi,* Corti, 1977, 95–112.

26 *Revue d'Histoire Littéraire de la France,* 71ᵉ année, No. 2, mars–avril 1971, 226–46. This is a useful article, although I am able to find little evidence for the schism mentioned in the title.

27 Comparable imagery is to be found in a number of earlier poems of Mallarmé, including the remarkable 'occasional' sonnet, 'Dans le jardin', which has recently been discovered and published. (See Eileen Holt and L. J. Austin, 'Stéphane Mallarmé: "Dans le Jardin"', *French Studies,* Vol. XXIX, No. 4, October 1975, 411–20.)

28 See below, pp. 80–81.

29 *Oxford Lectures on Poetry,* Macmillan, 1909, 191.

30 *O.c.,* 257.

31 *O.c.,* 260.

32 For a delightful self-parody, see Mallarmé's 'Prose pour Cazalis' (*O.c., 170*):

...

Et dans son extase
Le soleil riant
Fulgore Anastase
C'est tout l'Orient.

Et que nul ne rie
D'un rictus amer
Fleuris Pulchérie
Au bord de la mer

...

33 D. J. Mossop has written as follows in his invaluable *Pure Poetry. Studies in French Poetic Theory and Practice 1746 to 1945*, Oxford, Clarendon Press, 1971 : '...there is little or nothing to cushion the shock that the reader may experience when he comes into contact with words whose "inégalité" is so marked as to make for bewilderment, and whose beauty as "pierreries" may seem as forbiddingly austere as that of Mallarmé's Hérodiade. A very relevant example is provided by the "Prose pour des Esseintes", where the difficulty lies less in changes from one level of meaning to another than in a fundamental obscurity which results in an apparent incoherence and, in parts where the "inégalité" is less pronounced, an apparent flatness and barrenness.' (156)

34 *Vie de Mallarmé*, Gallimard, 1941, 450.

35 'Andrew Marvell', *Selected Essays*, Faber and Faber, 1934, 296.

36 *Peri Bathous* or *The Art of Sinking in Poetry*, reprinted in facsimile, ed. Edna Leake Steeves, New York, King's Crown Press, Columbia University, 1952, 69.

37 For an excellent account of Mallarmé's vocabulary, and of the creative role of his syntax, see Jacques Scherer, *L'Expression littéraire dans l'œuvre de Mallarmé*, Droz, 1947, 65 ff. René Ghil reports a conversation in which Mallarmé declared : '...il convient de nous servir des mots de tout le monde, dans le sens que tout le monde croit comprendre! Je n'emploie que ceux-là. Ce sont les mots mêmes que le Bourgeois lit tous les matins, les mêmes! Mais, voilà [...] s'il lui arrive de les retrouver en tel mien poème, il ne les comprend plus! C'est qu'ils ont été récrits par un poète.' (*Les Dates et les Œuvres*, Éditions G. Crès et Cie, 1923, 214–15). Horace made this point pithily in the *Ars Poetica*, lines 47–8. For a collection of Mallarmé's (and others') statements on syntax, and a review of his main syntactic innovations, see Robert Gibson, *Modern French Poets on Poetry*, Cambridge University Press, 1961, 157–63.

38 *Seven Types of Ambiguity*, Chatto and Windus, 1947, 211. On the psychic mechanism involved here, see Freud's 'Negation', The Standard Edition, Vol. xix, ed. James Strachey, The Hogarth Press, 1961, 235–9.

39 *O.c.*, 55. Comparable instances in the shorter poems are examined by David H. T. Scott in his penetrating study of 'Mallarmé and the Octosyllabic Sonnet', *French Studies*, Vol. xxxi, No. 2, April 1977, 149–63.

40 This enactment of mental process is one of many mimetic functions performed by Mallarmé's syntax. These functions have been overshadowed by the view, persuasively asserted by Valéry, which holds Mallarmé's syntax to be 'like mathematics' in its internal operations and its effects on the reading mind. (See Valéry, *Œuvres*, Vol. I, ed. Jean Hytier,

'Bibliothèque de la Pléiade', Gallimard, 1957, 658, 685;
Donald Davie (*Articulate Energy*, Routledge and Kegan Paul,
1955, 91–2), taking the first of these passages as his authority,
claims that *'poetic syntax is like mathematics when its function
is to please us in and for itself'* and that Mallarmé's 'appeals to
nothing but itself, to nothing outside the world of the poem'.)
Mallarmé's handling of syntax is far too varied to allow either
the mimetic or the mathematical view to be solely right.

41 Barbara Herrnstein Smith writes in her *Poetic Closure*,
University of Chicago Press, 1968: '. . .a certain degree of
syntactic chaos and structural incoherence can suggest the
internal reality, but poetry cannot attempt to be faithful to
the minutiae of interior verbalisation—not if it is to be
poetry.' (140)

42 For an admirably perceptive account of ambiguous syntax
as a source of metaphorical suggestion, see Christopher
Ricks, *Milton's Grand Style*, Oxford, Clarendon Press, 1963,
94ff and *passim*.

43 See *Die philosophischen Schriften*, ed. C. I. Gerhardt, Berlin,
1875–90 (Vol. VII, 289–91, and elsewhere). For a brief account
of the notion of 'compossibility' see *The Monadology and
Other Philosophical Writings*, translated and introduced by
Robert Latta, Oxford, Clarendon Press, 1898, 63–7.

44 *A la recherche du temps perdu*, ed. Pierre Clarac and André Ferré,
Vol. 1, 'Bibliothèque de la Pléiade', Gallimard, 1954, 229.

45 Mallarmé is a master in the joint manipulation of the two
sentence-types which Pater characterised as follows in his
essay on 'Style': 'The blithe, crisp sentence, decisive as a
child's expression of its needs, may alternate with the long-
contending, victoriously intricate sentence; the sentence, born
with the integrity of a single word, relieving the sort of sentence
in which, if you look closely, you can see much contrivance,
much adjustment, to bring a highly qualified matter into
compass at one view.' (*Appreciations*, Macmillan, 1889,
19–20.)

46 Jean-Pierre Richard has elegantly characterised this double
movement in his *L'Univers imaginaire de Mallarmé*, Seuil,
1961: 'Au monde de l'indétermination première – dans une
version primitive l'hyperbole était dite "indéfinissable" –
s'oppose celui de la détermination seconde, de la définition
consciente, qui refuse les risques d'une trop libre expansion.
[. . .] D'abord gonflée en une gloire, puis éployée en un
grandissement qui dépasse dangereusement les dimensions
de la raison et les possibilités de l'expression, la fleur est alors
ramenée sur terre, enclose dans les contours fixes d'une
œuvre, inscrite dans "d'éternels parchemins".' (401) On the
ambiguity of Marvell's 'The Garden', and the 'sense of
richness (readiness for argument not pursued)', in his

language, see William Empson, *Some Versions of Pastoral*,
Chatto and Windus, 1935, 118–45.

47 Troisième édition revue et augmentée, Champion, 1923, 35.

48 For Jean Cohen in his challenging and stimulating *Structure
du langage poétique*, Flammarion, 1966, the conflict between
metre and syntax in Mallarmé's verse places him at a
culminating point within a historical process ('une ligne
d'évolution, une sorte de loi tendancielle de la poésie
française'): '. . .au cours de ces trois périodes [i.e. Classicism,
Romanticism, Symbolism] de son histoire, la versification
n'a pas cessé d'accroître la divergence entre le mètre et la
syntaxe, *elle est allée toujours plus loin dans le sens de l'agram-
maticalisme.*' (69) Important reservations on Cohen's choice
of 'periods' and on other methodological matters are
expressed by Gérard Genette in his excellent review-article
'Langage poétique, poétique du langage', in *Figures 11*,
Seuil, 1969, 123–53.

49 See below, pp. 83–9. Hopkins, in his comments on a
metrical effect (reversal of stress in two consecutive feet),
evoked this general sensation of double rhythm with
remarkable force: 'If however the reversal is repeated in two
feet running, especially so as to include the sensitive second
foot, it must be due either to great want of ear or else is a
calculated effect, the superinducing or *mounting* of a new
rhythm upon the old; and since the new or mounted rhythm
is actually heard and at the same time the mind naturally
supplies the natural or standard foregoing rhythm, for we do
not forget what the rhythm is that by rights we should be
hearing, two rhythms are in some manner running at once
and we have something answerable to counterpoint in
music. . .' (*The Poems of Gerard Manley Hopkins*, Fourth
Edition, ed. W. H. Gardner and N. H. MacKenzie, Oxford
University Press, 1967, 46).

50 The reader is likely, of course, to dwell most upon those
formal features of the poem which do most semantic work.
Winifred Nowottny writes in her indispensable *The Language
Poets Use*, The Athlone Press, 1962: '[. . .] we probably tend to
pick out from among the myriad events occurring in a stream
of verse those which most successfully 'enact' the sense; we
disregard the irrelevant aspects of the total particularity of
what is occurring. [. . .] We need not, then, try to imagine a
state of affairs in which constantly and without intermission
the verse structure must particularize the sense of all that is
said in it; there may be much to be gained in calling upon it to
do this only at important points. Indeed it may be true that
what we feel as the inner movement of a poem may be
discernible to us chiefly because the poet controls that movement, by concentrating the force of the verse structure, and

the several powers it holds, at decisive nodal points where the
flow of meanings turns another way [. . .].' (116–17)
51 In *Style in Language*, ed. Thomas A. Sebeok, Cambridge, Mass.,
  M.I.T. Press, 1960, 350–77.
52 Jakobson, 'Linguistics and Poetics', 358.
53 Jakobson, 'Linguistics and Poetics', 368–9. The passage of
  Hopkins to which Jakobson refers is to be found in 'On
  the Origin of Beauty: a Platonic Dialogue', in *The Note-
  Books and Papers of Gerard Manley Hopkins*, ed. Humphry
  House, Oxford University Press, 1937, 80.
54 Jakobson, 'Linguistics and Poetics', 372, 370. For further
  statements and applications of Jakobson's theory of poetry,
  see ' "Les Chats" de Charles Baudelaire' (with Claude Lévi-
  Strauss), *L'Homme*, t.2, 1962, 5–21 (the prolonged critical-
  ideological debate to which this now celebrated article gave
  rise is reviewed in detail by Claude Pichois in his edition of
  Baudelaire's *Œuvres complètes*, Vol. 1, 'Bibliothèque de la
  Pléiade', Gallimard, 1975, 951–6); 'Poetry of Grammar and
  Grammar of Poetry', *Lingua*, Vol. 21, 1968, 597–609;
  Shakespeare's Verbal Art in 'Th'expence of Spirit' (with
  Lawrence G. Jones), The Hague, Mouton, 1970. These and a
  generous selection from Jakobson's other writings on poetry
  and poetics are now available in French, in *Questions de
  poétique*, Seuil, 1973. Comparable approaches of particular
  interest are to be found in Samuel R. Levin's *Linguistic
  Structures in Poetry*, The Hague, Mouton, 1962 and Nicolas
  Ruwet's *Langage, musique, poésie*, Seuil, 1972. For intelligent
  critiques of Jakobson's views, see Michael Riffaterre, *Essais de
  stylistique structurale*, Flammarion, 1971, 307–64, and Jonathan
  Culler, *Structuralist Poetics*, Routledge and Kegan Paul,
  1975, 55–74.
55 I am much indebted in this and other sections of the present
  study to Barbara Herrnstein Smith's excellent *Poetic Closure*
  (see note 41 above). Her modest subtitle 'a study of how
  poems end' does less than justice to a book which is in fact
  an unusually trenchant account of 'what poems are'.
56 On the memorability of verse as a product of sound-sense
  'couplings', see Samuel R. Levin, *Linguistic Structures in Poetry*,
  The Hague, Mouton, 1962, 39, 60–2.
57 *Le Vers français*, 226.
58 *La Légende des Siècles*, ed. Jacques Truchet, 'Bibliothèque de la
  Pléiade', Gallimard, 1950, 25.
59 In *Style in Language*, ed. Thomas A. Sebeok, Cambridge, Mass.,
  M.I.T. Press, 1960, 109–31.
60 Ibid., 118ff.
61 'On Musicality in Verse', in *The Philosophy of Literary Form*,
  Second Edition, Baton Rouge, Louisiana State University
  Press, 1967, 369–78. See also Roy Lewis, 'The Rhythmical

Creation of Beauty', *Forum for Modern Language Studies*, Vol. VI, No. 2, April 1970, 114ff.

62 My statistical survey has been far from rigorous, but it is interesting to note that in equivalent lengths from the three poems I took as a random sample – Lamartine's 'La Source dans les bois d***' (*Œuvres poétiques complètes*, ed. M.-F. Guyard, 'Bibliothèque de la Pléiade', Gallimard, 1963, 352–4), Hugo's '*Cæruleum Mare*' (*Œuvres poétiques*, ed. P. Albouy, Vol. 1, 'Bibliothèque de la Pléiade', Gallimard, 1964, 1110–12) and Valéry's 'Ébauche d'un serpent' (*Œuvres*, ed. J. Hytier, Vol. 1, 'Bibliothèque de la Pléiade', Gallimard, 1957, 138–9) – the totals are 9, 8 and 11 respectively.

63 *O.c.*, 387. In a letter to Stuart Merrill, Mallarmé commented as follows upon the power of concealed alliteration: 'J'ai même noté, au cours de plusieurs lectures, que vous êtes déjà, ce qui est l'art suprême, à dissimuler les jeux allitératifs, que trop de saisissable extériorité trahirait jusqu'au procédé, pour que le miracle du vers demeure, un instant, inexplicable. Allez dans ce sens.' (*Correspondance*, Vol. III, 1886–1889, ed. Henri Mondor and Lloyd James Austin, Gallimard, 1969, 111.)

64 In the earlier version of the poem (see Appendix) these lines contained an additional sibilant and two further alliterative elements: 'Que, sol des cent i*r*is, son si*t*e, / Ils savent s'il a, *c*er*t*e, é*t*é.' The removal of such correspondences from one version of a poem to the next is unusual. On assonances and/or alliterations *added* to create richer sound-patterning, see Alison Fairlie's ' "Mène-t-on la foule dans les ateliers?" ' – *Some Remarks on Baudelaire's Variants'*, *Order and Adventure in Post-Romantic French Poetry. Essays presented to C. A. Hackett*, ed. E. M. Beaumont, J. M. Cocking and J. Cruickshank, Oxford, Blackwell, 1973, 19, 23.

65 *Andromaque*, Act 5, v.

66 'Fragments du Narcisse', *Œuvres*, ed. Jean Hytier, Vol. 1, 'Bibliothèque de la Pléiade', Gallimard, 1957, 125.

67 Mallarmé himself made it plain that music was valuable to him, in thinking about poetry, not as *euphony* but as *structure*, as *organised relationship*. The following are among his best-known statements on the subject: 'les choses existent, nous n'avons pas à les créer; nous n'avons qu'à en saisir les rapports; et ce sont les fils de ces rapports qui forment les vers et les orchestres.' ('Réponse à Jules Huret', *O.c.*, 871); 'ce n'est pas de sonorités élémentaires par les cuivres, les cordes, les bois, indéniablement mais de l'intellectuelle parole à son apogée que doit avec plénitude et évidence, résulter, en tant que l'ensemble des rapports existant dans tout, la Musique.' ('Crise de vers', *O.c.*, 367–8). The role of musical concepts and models within Mallarmé's poetics has been examined with

great care by Suzanne Bernard in her *Mallarmé et la Musique*,
Nizet, 1959; see also Judy Kravis, *The Prose of Mallarmé*,
Cambridge University Press, 1976, 202–14 and *passim*.

68 Troisième édition, Payot, 1972, 235. For Freud's account of
pleasure in jokes, word-play and rhyme as deriving from 'an
economy of psychical expenditure', see *Jokes and their Relation
to the Unconscious*, The Standard Edition, Vol. VIII, ed. James
Strachey, The Hogarth Press, 1960, 117–26.

69 Aragon put the matter thus in his preface to *Les Yeux d'Elsa*,
London, Éditions Horizon-La France Libre, 1943: '. . . il n'y
a poésie qu'autant qu'il y a méditation sur le langage, et à
chaque pas réinvention de ce langage. Ce qui implique de
briser les cadres fixes du langage, les règles de la grammaire,
les lois du discours.' (xi)

70 *Précis de sémantique française*, Berne, Éditions Francke, 1952, 235.

71 *Les Faictz et Dictz de Jean Molinet*, ed. Noël Dupire, Vol. 2,
Société des Anciens Textes Français, 1937, 838. These lines are
from a flamboyant epistolary exchange with Cretin, for the
opening of which see below, p. 67; the first three of Molinet's
lines are quoted by Ullmann, *Précis de sémantique française*, 234.

72 The homonymic rhymes *pas : pas* and *nom : non* both occur in
'Toast funèbre'; the final couplet of the same poem rhymes on
nuit (O.c., 55). Mallarmé's boldest experiment with homonyms
in the rhyme position is to be found in the sonnet to Puvis de
Chavannes *(gourde:gourde, sourde:sourde) (O.c.,* 72).

73 *O.c.*, 367.

74 Selections from Saussure's notebooks are presented and
commented upon by Jean Starobinski in his *Les mots sous les
mots: les anagrammes de Ferdinand de Saussure*, Gallimard, 1971.

75 Starobinski, *Les mots sous les mots*, 153–4. Roman Jakobson
comments on Saussure's 'dichotomie factice du fortuit et du
prémédité' and on the decisive role of subliminal intention in
the creation of poetic structure, in *Questions de poétique*, Seuil,
1973, 198ff.

76 *Petit traité de poésie française* (1871), reprinted in *Œuvres*,
Lemerre, 1891, 52ff, 268. Banville's remarks on rhyme are still
among the subtlest and clearest-headed that we have.

77 Cf. the following representative remarks, from the works of
three of Mallarmé's most sensitive commentators: '[. . .] *Prose*
est le moment où la technique déborde l'émotion et devient
agressive' (Émilie Noulet, *L'Œuvre poétique de Stéphane
Mallarmé*, Droz, 1940, 255); 'There is a richness of rhymes
[. . .] that at times becomes sheer *coquetterie* (or deliberate
extravagance, to show up the defects of excessive method?)'
(A. R. Chisholm, *Mallarmé's 'Grand Œuvre'*, Manchester, The
University Press, 1962, 37–8); '[. . .] à travers tant de conditions prosodiques et sonores, le sens devient ce qu'il peut.'
(Pierre-Olivier Walzer, 'Prolégomènes à toute exégèse future

de la "Prose" ', *Festgabe Hans von Greyerz, zum sechzigsten Geburtstag, 5. April 1967*, Bern, Herbert Lang, 1967, 814).

78 Thibaudet writes briefly on Mallarmé's use of the *rime équivoque* in *La Poésie de Stéphane Mallarmé*, Gallimard, 1926, 241ff. On Baudelaire's *un*enthusiasm for the devices of the *rhétoriqueurs*, see Graham Chesters, *Some Functions of Sound-repetition in 'Les Fleurs du Mal'*, Occasional Papers in Modern Languages, No. 11, Hull, University of Hull Publications, 1975, 21–2. Chesters notes that it could be argued that the task of resurrecting these devices 'was fulfilled by Mallarmé and Valéry.' (22)

79 See *La Deffence et illustration de la langue francoyse*, ed. Henri Chamard, *Société des textes français modernes*, Didier, 1948, 145–6. Cf. Coleridge's remark: 'Double and tri-syllable rhymes, indeed, form a lower species of wit, and, attended to exclusively for their own sake, may become a source of momentary amusement [. . .]' (*Biographia Literaria*, ed. J. Shawcross, Vol. 11, Oxford University Press, 1907, 52).

80 *Œuvres poétiques*, ed. Kathleen Chesney, Firmin-Didot, 1932, 320. For a sympathetic view of the *rhétoriqueurs* and a useful history of the collective term, see Pierre Jodogne, 'Les "rhétoriqueurs" et l'humanisme: problème d'histoire littéraire', in *Humanism in France*, ed. A. H. T. Levi, Manchester, The University Press, 1970, 150–75.

81 Rabelais, *Œuvres*, ed. Abel Lefranc, Vol. 2, Champion, 1913, 411–12. On word-play in medieval verse, see Paul Zumthor, *Langue, texte, énigme*, Seuil, 1975.

82 On the authorship of this couplet, see Henri Morier, *Dictionnaire de poétique et de rhétorique*, Presses Universitaires de France, 1961, 350–1. Mallarmé was an admirer of Banville's prowess in rhyme, and wrote of *Le Forgeron*: '[. . .] la rime ici extraordinaire parce qu'elle ne fait qu'un avec l'alexandrin qui, dans ses poses et la multiplicité de son jeu, semble par elle dévoré tout entier comme si cette fulgurante cause de délice y triomphait jusqu'à l'initiale syllabe [. . .]' ('Solennité', *O.c.*, 332). On Mallarmé's admiration for Banville, see Judy Kravis, *The Prose of Mallarmé*, Cambridge University Press, 1976, 15–17.

83 For a persuasive account of phonetic patterning as play, and of the rich imaginative rewards offered by such play, see Roy Lewis, 'The Rhythmical Creation of Beauty', *Forum for Modern Language Studies*, Vol. VI, No. 2, April 1970, 106–7.

84 *Poems* and *A Defence of Ryme*, ed. Arthur Colby Sprague, Phoenix Books, University of Chicago Press, 1965, xxiii, 134.

85 i.e. they defend the metrical integrity of the line in the face of internal attack. W. Th. Elwert writes, in his paper on 'Mallarmé entre la tradition et le vers libre: ce qu'en disent ses *vers de circonstance*' (in *Le Vers français au 20e siècle*, ed. Monique Parent, Actes et colloques, 5, Klincksieck, 1967,

123–40): 'C'est que Mallarmé a mis un frein puissant à la dissolution du vers par le poids qu'il conférait à la rime. Plus il prenait de libertés avec l'unité syntaxique et rythmique du vers, plus il soulignait l'unité du vers en marquant nettement sa fin par la rime, moyen traditionnel non pas uniquement comme un artifice en soi [. . .] mais bien en fonction du vers et par rapport à l'enjambement.' (137) On 'conservative' and 'radical' elements within Mallarmé's versification, see Albert Thibaudet, *La Poésie de Stéphane Mallarmé*, Gallimard, 1926, 290–9.

86 His best-known and most sustained venture of this kind is to be found in the sonnet 'Le vierge, le vivace. . .' (*O.c.*, 67–8).

87 These and other means by which rhyme proper may be reinforced by 'informal, inessential sound-repetition' have been analysed by Graham Chesters in his excellent *Some Functions of Sound-repetition in 'Les Fleurs du Mal'*, Occasional Papers in Modern Languages, No. 11, Hull, University of Hull Publications, 1975, 9ff. Chesters comments: 'The principle of reinforcement is Baudelaire's answer to the problem of using a very rich rhyme without its becoming playful. Ultra-rich rhymes tend to be excessively conspicuous and, if used too freely, annihilate a sensitive response to the imagery and thought; Baudelaire avoids this danger by extending the rhyme in a very free and informal manner. At the same time, he strengthens the effect of symmetry and regular rhythm.' (14)

88 For a brief account of the semantic functions of rhyme, see René Wellek and Austin Warren, *Theory of Literature*, Third Edition, Harmondsworth, Peregrine Books, 1963, 160–1.

89 The paper first appeared in 1944 and is reprinted in *The Verbal Icon*, Lexington, University of Kentucky Press, 1954, 152–66.

90 Wimsatt, *The Verbal Icon*, 153, 156. The 'separatist' view is present in an extreme form in Marcelle Blum's *Le Thème symbolique dans le théâtre de Racine*, 2 vols, Nizet, 1962, 1965.

91 'Billet à Whistler', *O.c.*, 65.

92 'Au seul souci de voyager', *O.c.*, 72.

93 'Toute l'âme résumée', *O.c.*, 73. For Jean Cohen in his *Structure du langage poétique* (see note 48 above) such instances as these are the culmination of the 'agrammatical' tendency of French verse (65–72).

94 The productivity of the end-rhymes is thrown into further relief by the semantic poverty of the fore-rhymes which counterbalance many of them (see pp. 60–2 above).

95 See above, p. 55.

96 Winifred Nowottny has written persuasively on this capacity of complex literary devices such as rhyme 'to impede our tendency to reduce meaning to conceptual schemata': '[. . .] if the common procedures of conveying and interpreting

meaning are complicated by some device that is formative of
meaning in its own way, this 'interference' with our easy,
automatic processes of getting the meaning out of words
presents us, as it were, with the incentive to relate meanings to
one another in a heightened state of mental activity. This
'interference' is not an obstacle to understanding but a
challenge or an invitation to take a new route to understanding.' (*The Language Poets Use*, 142).

97 I have assumed here and elsewhere that, although each member of the rhyme-pair absorbs something of the other's meaning, the second, by completing the phonetic pattern and
occupying a later position within the syntactic sequence, is
dominant. None of Mallarmé's rhyme-pairs in 'Prose' involves
words from different sentences.

98 For a brief account of the problem, see Otto Jespersen, *The
Philosophy of Grammar*, Allen and Unwin, 1924, 92–5. My
examples are from among those given by Jespersen.

99 Other factors deserve to be mentioned as (possibly) contribut-
ing to this subliminal sense of triumph. The genitives which
figure prominently elsewhere in the poem are absent from the
last four quatrains: the atmosphere of caution produced by
the repeated subordination of attribute to object, or of one
object to another, has disappeared. The syntactic parallelism
of 13.3 and 14.3 gives these lines a power of persuasion that
the much-qualified sentences in which they appear could
alone scarcely grant them. This is an instance of the verse-
feature Donald Davie calls 'syntax as rhyme' (*Articulate
Energy*, Routledge and Kegan Paul, 1955, 91), here superinduced upon an already prominent rhyme-structure.

100 'par chemins' = *per* + Vulgar Latin *camminus*. 'parchemins' =
Latin adj. *pergamena*, from the equivalent Greek (of, or
pertaining to, Pergamum, the city in Asia Minor).

101 Faber and Faber, 1964, 432. For a comparative study of the
two writers' techniques of word-play (with special reference
to *Un Coup de dés* and *Finnegans Wake*), and a collection of
Mallarmean references and echoes in the work of Joyce, see
David Hayman, *Joyce et Mallarmé*, 2 vols, Collection 'Confrontations' No. 2, Lettres Modernes, 1956.

102 See above, p. 30.

103 The emergence and consolidation of the theory are discussed
by J. E. Raven in his admirable *Plato's Thought in the Making*,
Cambridge University Press, 1965.

104 The philosophical seriousness of this dialogue has been dis-
puted; it has been defended by, among many others, Gilbert
Ryle, *Collected Papers*, Vol. 1, Hutchinson, 1971, 1–44, and
J. E. Raven, *Plato's Thought in the Making*, 203–24. Raven
writes: '[. . .] whatever objective validity any of Parmenides'
criticisms may possess, Plato himself, who either invented

them or borrowed them from his critics, somehow managed
to remain undismayed.' (217)
105 See above, pp. 34–5.
106 Although Plato raises the question on a number of occasions,
there is little evidence to suggest that he himself would ever
have answered it otherwise than affirmatively. See W. D.
Ross, *Plato's Theory of Ideas*, Oxford, Clarendon Press, 1951, 15.
107 *Œuvres*, ed. Jean Hytier, Vol. II, 'Bibliothèque de la Pléiade',
Gallimard, 1960, 213.
108 See, for example, *Laws* 654A, 816B, 957C, 960C.
109 The *Phaedrus* is perhaps the dialogue richest in effects of this
kind; see, for example, 237A, 238C, 244C and *passim*. R.
Hackforth, commenting on the first of these, speaks of 'those
etymological jests in which Plato often, and sometimes rather
pointlessly, indulges' (*Plato's Phaedrus*, Cambridge University
Press, 1952, 36). Elsewhere the same author remarks: 'Plato
is ready to accept or reject popular etymologies according as
they do or do not suit his momentary purpose. The etymology
of "Hades" here [*Phaedo* 80D] accepted is rejected at *Cratylus*
404B.' (*Plato's Phaedo*, Cambridge University Press, 1955, 88).
110 Victor Goldschmidt gives a brief history of the predecessors
to whose thought on language Plato alludes, in his *Essai sur le
"Cratyle"* (Bibliothèque de l'École des Hautes Études, No.
279), Champion, 1940, 5–35.
111 On the sign as arbitrary or unmotivated, see *Cours de linguistique générale*, Payot, 1972, 100–2. Émile Benveniste
proposes a more restricted definition of this arbitrariness in
his *Problèmes de linguistique générale* [1], Gallimard, 1966, 49–55.
112 'Proust et les noms', in *Le Degré zéro de l'écriture* suivi de
Nouveaux essais critiques, 'Points', Seuil, 1972, 134.
113 Seuil, 1976. On Mallarmé, see 257–78 and *passim*. In one of
the articles from which the larger study grew ('Avatars du
cratylisme', *Poétique*, No. 11, 1972, 367–94) Genette speaks of
'une attitude somme toute assez répandue, de Platon à
Mallarmé (et au-delà), et qu'on pourrait baptiser paraphrasti-
quement cratylisme impur, si quelques raisons ne militaient
en faveur d'une autre désignation, peut-être provisoire: celle
de *cratylisme secondaire*.' He continues: 'le cratylisme *primaire*
consiste non seulement à valoriser l'hypothèse d'un mimé-
tisme linguistique et à attribuer aux éléments, phoniques et/ou
graphiques, de la langue une telle capacité mimétique, mais
encore à considérer que les mots de la langue sont effective-
ment constitués selon cette capacité [...] c'est évidemment le
cratylisme proprement dit, celui de Cratyle lui-même, pour
qui tous les noms sont justes et bien formés. Le cratylisme
secondaire, plus exigeant ou plus réaliste, s'annonce d'une
certaine manière chez le Socrate du dialogue éponyme. Il
répond généralement aux deux premiers critères, mais il

décline le troisième, reconnaissant non sans regret que les mots ne sont pas toujours constitués conformément aux valeurs symboliques qu'il attribue lui-même aux éléments de la langue: ainsi Socrate critiquant le *l* et le *s* de *sklérotès* ou Mallarmé déplorant les sonorités "inverses" d'*ombre* et *ténèbres*, de *jour* et *nuit*. Ce qui invite à baptiser une telle attitude cratylisme *secondaire*, c'est qu'au contraire de l'hermogénisme pur et simple, qui s'en tient, satisfait ou résigné, à un conventionalisme radical et sans (a)ménagements, elle cherche souvent à dépasser ce constat de carence. Jugeant la langue "imparfaite", mais perfectible dans le sens d'une plus grande mimésis, elle souhaite la corriger d'une manière ou d'une autre.' (393–4)

114 *O.c.*, 364. For a comparative account of Mallarmé and Plato on language, see Guy Delfel, *L'Esthétique de Stéphane Mallarmé*, Flammarion, 1951, 134–57. Delfel writes of the ending of the *Cratylus*: 'Mallarmé se sépare ici de Platon. Alors que celui-ci abandonnait le langage pour fonder la Science sur une autre technique, Mallarmé va chercher à remédier aux défauts du langage que nous avons énumérés. Il rêve d'une transmutation du langage qui le rendra propre à saisir enfin *matériellement la vérité*, ou, du moins, à la suggérer' (149). See also Maurice Blanchot, *L'Espace littéraire*, Gallimard, 1955, 30–6 and 'Le Mythe de Mallarmé', *La Part du feu*, Gallimard, 1949, 35–48.

115 See Goldschmidt, *Essai sur le "Cratyle"*, 28–9.

116 See above, pp. 23–4.

117 On Mallarmé's botany, see L. J. Austin, 'Mallarmé and the "Prose pour des Esseintes" ', *Forum for Modern Language Studies*, Vol. II, No. 3, July 1966, 206–8. The author points out that Mallarmé's inclusion of the lily among the *iridaceae* is less unorthodox than it may seem, if we remember that the heraldic *fleur de lys* is the *Iris pseudacorus*.

118 *Science and the Modern World*, Cambridge University Press, 1926, 44.

119 *Seven Types of Ambiguity*, Second Edition, Chatto and Windus, 1947, 192.

120 Ibid., 226. For Freud's account of the reconciliation of opposites within the dream-work, see *The Interpretation of Dreams*, The Standard Edition of the Complete Psychological Works, ed. James Strachey, Hogarth Press, 1953, Vol. IV, 316–19, Vol. V, 596–7, etc.

121 Éditions de Minuit, 1972, 37, 61.

122 Seuil, 1974, 219. Those unfamiliar with this general approach to the study of poetic texts will find a helpful introduction in Ivan Fónagy's paper on 'The Functions of Vocal Style' (in *Literary Style: a Symposium*, ed. Seymour Chatman, Oxford University Press, 1971, 159–74). Kristeva's detailed account of 'Prose' (*La Révolution du langage poétique*, 239 ff), which is

based upon a 'semi-phonological' transcription of the text, cannot usefully be read in isolation from the extended chapter in which it occurs ('Rythmes phoniques et sémantiques', 209–63): her analysis deals at length with the irruptions of the 'dispositif sémiotique', but scarcely at all with the symbolic codes which these drives deflect, and are deflected by, within the poetic text (these codes are dealt with in the theoretical part of the chapter).

123 Ibid. Kristeva's preface ends as follows: 'Ce que nous désignons par *signifiance* est précisément cet engendrement illimité et jamais clos, ce fonctionnement sans arrêt des pulsions vers, dans et à travers le langage, vers, dans et à travers l'échange et ses protagonistes: le sujet et ses institutions. Ce procès hétérogène, ni fond morcelé anarchique, ni blocage schizophrène, est une *pratique* de structuration et de déstructuration, passage à la *limite* subjective et sociale, et – à cette condition seulement – il est jouissance et révolution.' (15)

124 *Paysage de Chateaubriand*, Seuil, 1967, 162.

CHAPTER THREE

1 *Œuvres*, ed. Jean Hytier, Vol. 1, 'Bibliothèque de la Pléiade', Gallimard, 1957, 624–5. In my references to *Un Coup de dés* I shall use the numerals 1–11 to specify the relevant double page of the original single-volume edition (Gallimard, 1914), reproduced on pp. 93–113 of the present volume.

2 Mallarmé himself thought of the 'ideographic' character of the poem as a significant part of his achievement. In a letter to Gide he wrote: 'Je vous enverrai à Florence, d'où cela peut vous suivre autre part, la première épreuve convenable. La constellation y affectera, d'après des lois exactes, et autant qu'il est permis à un texte imprimé, fatalement une allure de constellation. Le vaisseau y donne de la bande, du haut d'une page au bas de l'autre, etc.; car, c'est là tout le point de vue (qu'il me fallait omettre dans un périodique) le rythme d'une phrase au sujet d'un acte ou même d'un objet n'a de sens que s'il les imite, et, figuré sur le papier, repris par la lettre, à l'estampe originelle, n'en sait rendre, malgré tout, quelque chose' (Quoted by Henri Mondor, *Vie de Mallarmé*, Gallimard, 1941, 770–1). For a brief and sympathetic view of Mallarmé's typography as pictorial imitation, see A. R. Chisholm, *Mallarmé's 'Grand Œuvre'*, Manchester, The University Press, 1962, 91–4. By far the most original mimetic readings of Mallarmé's lay-out are those by Claude Roulet and Ernest Fraenkel (see note 11 below). Fraenkel sets out to actualise the 'bel album d'imagerie abstraite' which Valéry saw in *Un Coup de dés* (*Œuvres*, Vol. 1, 627). For Fraenkel the under-

lying, unconscious drama of the poem is that of *being* itself: this drama is made visible by tracing out the zig-zag paths taken by the eye as it scans each of Mallarmé's double pages.

3 'Le papier intervient chaque fois qu'une image, d'elle-même, cesse ou rentre, acceptant la succession d'autres et, comme il ne s'agit pas, ainsi que toujours, de traits sonores réguliers ou vers – plutôt, de subdivisions prismatiques de l'Idée, l'instant de paraître et que dure leur concours, dans quelque mise en scène spirituelle exacte, c'est à des places variables, près ou loin du fil conducteur latent, en raison de la vraisemblance, que s'impose le texte. L'avantage, si j'ai droit à le dire, littéraire, de cette distance copiée qui mentalement sépare des groupes de mots ou les mots entre eux, semble d'accélérer tantôt et de ralentir le mouvement, le scandant, l'intimant même selon une vision simultanée de la Page: celle-ci prise pour unité comme l'est autre part le Vers ou ligne parfaite. La fiction affleurera et se dissipera, vite, d'après la mobilité de l'écrit, autour des arrêts fragmentaires d'une phrase capitale dès le titre introduite et continuée. Tout se passe par raccourci, en hypothèse; on évite le récit.' (*O.c.*, 455.)

4 For a concise introduction to the world of concrete poetry, see Stephen Bann's *Concrete Poetry: an international anthology*, London Magazine Editions, 1967. For an extended critical account, see Pierre Garnier, *Spatialisme et poésie concrète*, Gallimard, 1968.

5 *Œuvres poétiques*, ed. Marcel Adéma and Michel Décaudin, 'Bibliothèque de la Pléiade', Gallimard, 1965, 203.

6 *Spatialisme et poésie concrète*, 168–9.

7 The problem arises: 'what is a space?' As Mallarmé clearly intended each double page of the text to be read as a unit (see note 3 above), one might argue that the spaces offered by the central margins are present merely for the convenience of printer and binder and have no semantic weight. Yet these margins, which are a feature of all the main editions of the text, do introduce conspicuous breaks into the poem. It is difficult to imagine that these breaks, resembling as they do all the others in *Un Coup de dés*, can fail to affect the way we read it, even if we take a conscious, principled decision to ignore them. Besides, it could well be that Mallarmé's awareness of these central margins was a determining factor in his choice of lay-out, and that an edition which sought to eliminate them would be unfaithful to his intentions.

8 Many more cases of this kind arise if one treats the central margins of each double page as affording a series of properly 'semantic' spaces (see previous note). Gardner Davies writes: 'La disposition typographique adoptée par Mallarmé permet au lecteur de dégager les unités syntactiques, dont les plus longues sont imprimées dans un caractère particulier, tandis

que les plus courtes s'isolent grace aux "blancs" qui les
entourent. Tout en facilitant la décomposition des unités
syntactiques, cependant, la forme typographique du *Coup de
Dés* offre en outre l'avantage de scander le texte, situé à
mi-chemin entre le poème en prose et le vers libre' (*Vers une
explication rationnelle du 'Coup de Dés'*, Corti, 1953, 197). He
does not point out that Mallarmé's spacing is an *unreliable* aid
to syntactic analysis, nor that space cannot at the same time
serve this function and that of providing a 'poetic' scansion of
the text, without creating difficulty and tension.

9 IX, 1088–90. Christopher Ricks, to whom I owe the example,
gives four possible patterns for Milton's syntax in these lines,
and comments: 'All these cries are equally simple, but all are
slightly different. The punctuation selects from among them,
of course [. . .] But the effect of the two lines is as of innumerable cries, as of innumerable boughs, to innumerable trees –
all of which telescope into one terrifyingly simply cry.'
(*Milton's Grand Style*, Oxford, Clarendon Press, 1963, 83–4.)

10 Pierre Reverdy, *Main d'œuvre*, Mercure de France, 1949, 231.

11 *O.c.*, 27, 72, 76. On the relations between these sonnets and
Un Coup de dés, see Charles Chadwick, *Mallarmé. Sa pensée dans
sa poésie*, Corti, 1962, 128–56. Further accounts of the poem
(and/or relevant documents) are to be found in the works by
Goffin, Chisholm, Mossop, Kristeva and Verdin mentioned
above (p. 163, n. 22), and in the following books (among
many others): Maurice Blanchot, *L'Espace littéraire,* Gallimard,
1955, and *Le Livre à venir*, Gallimard, 1959; Yves Bonnefoy,
L'Improbable, Mercure de France, 1959 and *Le Nuage rouge*,
Mercure de France, 1977; R. G. Cohn, *Mallarmé's 'Un Coup
de Dés': an exegesis*, New Haven, Yale French Studies Publica-
tions, 1949, *L'Œuvre de Mallarmé: Un Coup de Dés*, Librairie
Les Lettres, 1951, and *Mallarmé's Masterwork. New Findings*,
Series Practica, 1, The Hague, Mouton, 1966; Guy Delfel,
L'Esthétique de Stéphane Mallarmé, Flammarion, 1951; Jacques
Derrida, *La Dissémination*, Seuil, 1972; Ernest Fraenkel, *Les
Dessins trans-conscients de Stéphane Mallarmé*, Nizet, 1960; Julia
Kristeva, 'Sémanalyse et production de sens, quelques
problèmes de sémiotique littéraire à propos d'un texte de
Mallarmé: *Un coup de dés. . .*', in *Essais de sémiotique poétique*,
ed. A. J. Greimas, Larousse, 1972; Charles Mauron,
Introduction à la psychanalyse de Mallarmé (1950), Neuchâtel,
A la Baconnière, new ed. 1968, and *Mallarmé par lui-même*,
Seuil, 1964; Émilie Noulet, *L'Œuvre poétique de Stéphane
Mallarmé*, Droz, 1940 (reprinted, Bruxelles, Éditions Jacques
Antoine, 1974); Claude Roulet, *Éléments de poétique
mallarméenne*, Neuchâtel, Éditions du Griffon, 1947, and *Traité
de poétique supérieure*, Neuchâtel, Éditions H. Messeiller, 1956;
Jean-Paul Sartre, *Situations*, IX, Gallimard, 1972. Jacques

Scherer, *Le 'Livre' de Mallarmé. Premières recherches sur des documents inédits*, Gallimard, 1957; Elizabeth Sewell, *The Structure of Poetry*, Routledge and Kegan Paul, 1951; Bernard Weinberg, *The Limits of Symbolism*, University of Chicago Press, 1966. In my own view, the most remarkable critical achievement remains Gardner Davies, *Vers une explication rationnelle du 'Coup de Dés'*, Corti, 1953. The author writes perceptively on all aspects of the poem, and provides a patient and practical key to its syntax (200–6). The reader is referred to this key for fuller information than my own argument requires. Although Davies's allegorising critical method is open to serious dispute, he uses it imaginatively throughout, and describes Mallarmé's art of plural suggestion much more fully than his title would seem to promise.

12 *O.c.*, 441.
13 On the interpretation of this sonnet see Gardner Davies, *Vers une explication rationnelle du 'Coup de Dés'*, Corti, 1953, 88–9, Émilie Noulet, *Vingt poèmes de Stéphane Mallarmé. Exégèses*, 'Textes littéraires français', Genève, Droz, 1967, 238–47 and Dorothy Gabe Coleman, *Maurice Scève: Poet of Love. Tradition and Originality*, Cambridge University Press, 1975, 3–13. Coleman tellingly portrays the gradual transition within the reader's mind from immediate musical impact to intellectual understanding. On the means by which Mallarmé achieves the extraordinarily concentrated suggestiveness of his octosyllabic sonnets, see David H. T. Scott's article mentioned above (Chapter Two, note 39).
14 *What is Art?* and *Essays on Art*, trans. Aylmer Maude, Oxford University Press, 1930, 167.
15 In *The Marriage of Heaven and Hell* (*The Complete Writings*, ed. Geoffrey Keynes, Oxford University Press, 1966, 148–58).
16 For Aristotle's summary of the Pythagoreans' view of number, see *Metaphysics A*5, 985b 23. This passage is quoted and discussed by G. S. Kirk and J. E. Raven in their *The Presocratic Philosophers*, Cambridge University Press, 1957, 236–50.
17 For a valuable introduction to the whole topic of number and the imagination, see Christopher Butler, *Number Symbolism*, Routledge and Kegan Paul, 1970.
18 *Œuvres complètes*, ed. Claude Pichois, Vol. 1, 'Bibliothèque de la Pléiade', Gallimard, 1975, 143. For other readings than my own of the last line, see the editor's note, 1115–16.
19 *O.c.*, 646.
20 The first three cases are commented upon by Gardner Davies (*Vers une explication rationnelle du 'Coup de Dés'*, 76–7).
21 *Glossaire j'y serre mes gloses* dates from 1939, and has been reprinted in *Mots sans mémoire*, Gallimard, 1969. *Biffures* (Gallimard, 1948) is the first volume of Leiris's autobiographical tetralogy *La Règle du jeu*.

22 See above, pp. 81–3. Gérard Genette has studied the 'cratylism' of Leiris in *Mimologiques*, Seuil, 1976, 315–75. See also Jeffrey Mehlman's outstanding *A Structural Study of Autobiography*, Cornell University Press, 1974, 100–35.

23 *Mots sans mémoire*, 75–112.

24 Mallarmé's proof-corrections to the so-called 'Lahure' edition would suggest that this contrast was an important part of his intention. The annotated and corrected proofs are reproduced by R. G. Cohn in his *Mallarmé's Masterwork. New Findings*, Series Practica, 1, The Hague, Mouton, 1966, 89–111. (The printer was not Lahure but Didot.)

25 'Isabella', *The Poetical Works*, ed. H. W. Garrod, Oxford University Press, 1956, 185.

26 Gallimard, 1959, 287. For a comparable approach, and a number of crucial insights into the role of *Un Coup de dés* within the development of modern poetry in Europe and the Americas, see Octavio Paz, *The Bow and the Lyre*, trans. Ruth L. C. Simms, McGraw-Hill, 1973, 249–54 and *passim*, and *Children of the Mire*, trans. Rachel Phillips, Harvard University Press, 1974, 112–14 and *passim*.

27 Blanchot, *Le Livre à venir*, 285–6. Roland Barthes has described the power of this same space to annihilate received meaning and ready-made literary effect: 'L'agraphie typo-graphique de Mallarmé veut créer autour des mots raréfiés une zone vide dans laquelle la parole, libérée de ses harmonies sociales et coupables, ne résonne heureusement plus. Le vocable, dissocié de la gangue des clichés habituels, des réflexes techniques de l'écrivain, est alors pleinement irresponsable de tous les contextes possibles ; il s'approche d'un acte bref, singulier, dont la matité affirme une solitude, donc une innocence.' (*Le Degré zéro de l'écriture* (1953), 'Points', Seuil, 1972, 55.)

28 For Einstein's account of his own and Descartes's reasons for rejecting the notion of empty space, see his *Relativity. The Special and the General Theory*, Methuen, 1954, 135–57.

CONCLUDING NOTE

1 *The Liberal Imagination* (1951), Harmondsworth, Peregrine Books, 1970, 289.

APPENDIX

1 An early version of the first twelve quatrains of 'Prose' (without title) was published from autograph MS. by Henri Mondor in *Le Figaro Littéraire*, 25 déc. 1954. The MS. was re-transcribed and discussed in detail by L. J. Austin in 'Du nouveau sur la "Prose pour des Esseintes" de Mallarmé',

Mercure de France, t. CCCXXIII, No. 1097, jan.–avril 1955, 84–104. Mondor's transcription is reprinted in his *Autres précisions sur Mallarmé et Inédits*, Gallimard, 1961, 141–3. A handwritten copy of this early version has since come to light. This copy, made by the Italian poet and novelist Luigi Gualdo, contains the two final quatrains previously missing. These were published by Charles Chadwick in 'Du nouveau sur "Prose pour des Esseintes"', *Revue d'Histoire Littéraire de la France*, 68ᵉ année, No. 1, jan.–fév. 1968, 87–8. The entire Gualdo copy was published and discussed by Carl Paul Barbier in his *Documents Stéphane Mallarmé I*, Nizet, 1968, 9–39. The version printed here reproduces Austin's transcription of the Mallarmé MS. (now modified from 'tiens' to 'siens' in 3.4) for quatrains 1–12 and the Gualdo copy (as published by Chadwick and Barbier) for quatrains 13–14. Oddities of spelling in the final quatrains are likely to have been introduced by the copyist.

LIST OF WORKS CITED

This list contains all the main primary and secondary works to which I have referred in my text and notes. I have excluded a number of literary or philosophical works, mentioned or alluded to above, which exist in readily available modern editions.

PRIMARY TEXTS

(a) *Works by Mallarmé*

Œuvres complètes, ed. Henri Mondor and G. Jean-Aubry, 'Bibliothèque de la Pléiade', Gallimard, 1951.

'Prose (pour des Esseintes)', *La Revue indépendante*, t.ii, no. 3, jan. 1885, 194–7.

Un Coup de dés jamais n'abolira le hasard, Gallimard, 1914.

Correspondance, Vol. i, 1862–71, ed. Henri Mondor and Jean-Pierre Richard, Gallimard, 1959.

   Vol. iii, 1886–9, ed. Henri Mondor and Lloyd James Austin, Gallimard, 1969.

(b) *Documentary Sources*

Austin, L. J., 'Du nouveau sur la "Prose pour des Esseintes" de Mallarmé', *Mercure de France*, t.cccxxiii, no. 1097, jan.–avril 1955, 84–104.

Barbier, Carl Paul, *Documents Stéphane Mallarmé I*, Nizet, 1968.

Chadwick, Charles, 'Du nouveau sur "Prose pour des Esseintes"', *Revue d'Histoire Littéraire de la France*, 68e année, no. 1, jan.–fév. 1968, 87–8.

Mondor, Henri, *Autres précisions sur Mallarmé et Inédits*, Gallimard, 1961.

   Vie de Mallarmé, Gallimard, 1941.

Scherer, Jacques, *Le 'Livre' de Mallarmé. Premières recherches sur des documents inédits*, Gallimard, 1957.

BOOKS ON MALLARMÉ

Barbier, Carl Paul, ed., *Colloque Mallarmé* (Glasgow, Novembre 1973) *en l'honneur de Austin Gill*, Nizet, 1975.

Bernard, Suzanne, *Mallarmé et la musique*, Nizet, 1959.

Boulay, Daniel, *L'Obscurité esthétique de Mallarmé et la 'Prose pour des Esseintes'*, chez l'auteur, 57 *bis*. av. de la Motte-Picquet, 1960.

Cellier, Léon, *Mallarmé et la morte qui parle*, Presses Universitaires de France, 1959.

Chadwick, Charles, *Mallarmé. Sa pensée dans sa poésie*, Corti, 1962.

Chisholm, A. R., *Mallarmé's 'Grand Œuvre'*, Manchester, The University Press, 1962.

Cohn, Robert Greer, *Mallarmé's 'Un Coup de Dés': an exegesis*, New Haven, Yale French Studies Publications, 1949.

L'Œuvre de Mallarmé: Un Coup de Dés, Librairie Les Lettres, 1951.

Toward the Poems of Mallarmé, Berkeley and Los Angeles, University of California Press, 1965.

Mallarmé's Masterwork. New Findings, Series Practica, 1, The Hague, Mouton, 1966.

Davies, Gardner, *Les 'Tombeaux' de Mallarmé*, Corti, 1950.

Vers une explication rationnelle du 'Coup de Dés', Corti, 1953.

Delfel, Guy, *L'Esthétique de Stéphane Mallarmé*, Flammarion, 1951.

Faure, Gabriel, *Mallarmé à Tournon*, Éditions des Horizons de France, 1946.

Fraenkel, Ernest, *Les Dessins trans-conscients de Stéphane Mallarmé*, Nizet, 1960.

Goffin, Robert, *Mallarmé vivant*, Nizet, 1956.

Hayman, David, *Joyce et Mallarmé*, 2 vols, Collection 'Confrontations' no. 2, Lettres Modernes, 1956.

Kravis, Judy, *The Prose of Mallarmé*, Cambridge University Press, 1976.

Mauron, Charles, *Introduction à la psychanalyse de Mallarmé* (1950), new ed., Neuchâtel, A la Baconnière, 1968.

Mallarmé par lui-même, Seuil, 1964.

Noulet, Émilie, *L'Œuvre poétique de Stéphane Mallarmé*, Droz, 1940 (reprinted, Bruxelles, Éditions Jacques Antoine, 1974).

Vingt poèmes de Stéphane Mallarmé. Exégèses, 'Textes littéraires français', Genève, Droz, 1967.

Richard, Jean-Pierre, *L'Univers imaginaire de Mallarmé*, Seuil, 1961.

Roulet, Claude, *Éléments de poétique mallarméenne*, Neuchâtel, Éditions du Griffon, 1947.

Traité de poétique supérieure, Neuchâtel, Éditions H. Messeiller, 1956.

Scherer, Jacques, *L'Expression littéraire dans l'œuvre de Mallarmé*, Droz, 1947.

Thibaudet, Albert, *La Poésie de Stéphane Mallarmé*, Gallimard, 1926.

Verdin, Simonne, *Stéphane Mallarmé, le presque contradictoire*, précédé d'une *Étude de variantes*, Nizet, 1975.

ARTICLES ON MALLARMÉ IN PERIODICALS AND COLLECTIVE VOLUMES

Austin, L. J., 'Mallarmé et le rêve du "Livre"', *Mercure de France*, t.CCCXVII, no. 1073, janvier 1953, 81–108.

'Mallarmé, Huysmans et la "Prose pour des Esseintes"', *Revue d'Histoire Littéraire de la France*, 54ᵉ année, no. 2, avril–juin 1954, 145–83.

'Du nouveau sur la "Prose pour des Esseintes" de Mallarmé', *Mercure de France*, t.cccxxiii, no. 1097, jan.–avril 1955, 84–104.

'Mallarmé and the "Prose pour des Esseintes"', *Forum for Modern Language Studies*, Vol. ii, no. 3, July 1966, 197–213.

'Mallarmé et le réel', in *Modern Miscellany* (presented to Eugène Vinaver), ed. T. E. Lawrenson, F. E. Sutcliffe, and G. F. A. Gadoffre, Manchester, The University Press, 1969, 12–24.

'Mallarmé's Reshaping of "Le Pitre châtié"', in *Order and Adventure in Post-Romantic French Poetry. Essays presented to C. A. Hackett*, ed. E. M. Beaumont, J. M. Cocking and J. Cruickshank, Oxford, Blackwell, 1973, 56–71.

Austin, L. J. and Holt, Eileen, 'Stéphane Mallarmé: "Dans le Jardin"', *French Studies*, Vol. xxix, no. 4, October 1975, 411–20.

Champigny, Robert, 'Mallarmé's Relation to Platonism and Romanticism', *The Modern Language Review*, Vol. li, no. 3, July 1956, 348–58.

'The *Swan* and the Question of Pure Poetry', *L'Esprit Créateur* (Special no. on Mallarmé), Vol. i, no. 3, Fall 1961, 145–55.

Chisholm, A. R., 'Mallarmé: "*Le vierge, le vivace . . .*"', *French Studies*, Vol. xvi, no. 4, October 1962, 359–63.

Cohen, Jean, 'L' "Obscurité" de Mallarmé', *Revue d'esthétique*, t.15, fasc. 1, jan.–mars 1962, 64–72.

Davies, Gardner, 'Stéphane Mallarmé: Fifty Years of Research', *French Studies*, Vol. i, no. 1, January 1947, 1–26.

Douchin, Jacques, 'La "Prose pour des Esseintes" ou l'examen de conscience de Mallarmé', *Orbis Litterarum* (Copenhagen), t.xvii, fasc. 1–2, 1962, 82–99.

Duchesne-Guillemin, Jacques, 'Sur la "Prose"', *Synthèses* (Bruxelles), 22e année, déc. 1967–jan. 1968, 57–60.

Dumas, Olivier, 'Mallarmé, Platon et "La Prose pour des Esseintes"', *Revue des sciences humaines*, no. 126, avril–juin 1967, 239–57.

Elwert, W. Th., 'Mallarmé entre la tradition et le vers libre: ce qu'en disent ses *vers de circonstance*', in *Le Vers français au 20e siècle*, ed. Monique Parent, Actes et Colloques, 5, Klincksieck, 1967, 123–40.

Gans, Eric, 'Prose poétique', *Romanic Review*, Vol. lxvi, no. 3, May 1975, 187–98.

Goffin, Robert, 'Rétrospections', *Synthesès* (Bruxelles), 22e année, déc. 1967–jan. 1968, 66–8.

Holt, Eileen and Austin, L. J., 'Stéphane Mallarmé: "Dans le Jardin"', *French Studies*, Vol. xxix, no. 4, October 1975, 411–20.

Kristeva, Julia, 'Sémanalyse et production de sens, quelques problèmes de sémiotique littéraire à propos d'un texte de Mallarmé: *Un coup de dés. . .*', *Essais de sémiotique poétique*, ed. A. J. Greimas, Larousse, 1972.

Mossop, D. J., 'Mallarmé's "Prose pour des Esseintes"', *French Studies*, Vol. xviii, no. 2, April 1964, 123–35.

Scott, David H. T., 'Mallarmé and the Octosyllabic Sonnet', *French Studies*, Vol. xxxi, no. 2, April 1977, 149–63.

Verdin, Simonne, '"Prose pour des Esseintes". Exégèse', *Revue de l'Université de Bruxelles*, 20e année, oct. 1967–jan. 1968, 122–46.

Verdin, Simonne, 'L'Action restreinte', *Synthèses* (Bruxelles), 22ᵉ année, déc. 1967–jan. 1968, 113–18.

Verhoeff, J. P., 'Anciens et modernes devant la "Prose pour des Esseintes"', *Revue d'Histoire Littéraire de la France*, 71ᵉ année, no. 2, mars–avril 1971, 226–46.

Walzer, Pierre-Olivier, 'Prolégoménes à toute exégèse future de la "Prose"', *Festgabe Hans von Greyerz, sum sechzigsten Geburtstag, 5. April 1967*, Bern, Herbert Lang, 1967, 809–15.

CRITICAL AND POLEMICAL WORKS INCLUDING
DISCUSSION OF MALLARMÉ

Barthes, Roland, *Le Degré zéro de l'écriture* (1953), suivi de *Nouveaux essais critiques*, 'Points', Seuil, 1972.

Béguin, Albert, *L'Ame romantique et le rêve* (1939), Corti, 1946.

Benda, Julien, *La France byzantine*, Gallimard, 1945.

Blanchot, Maurice, *Faux pas*, Gallimard, 1943.

La Part du feu, Gallimard, 1949.

L'Espace littéraire, Gallimard, 1955.

Le Livre à venir, Gallimard, 1959.

Bonnefoy, Yves, *L'Improbable*, Mercure de France, 1959.

Le Nuage rouge, Mercure de France, 1977.

Derrida, Jacques, *La Dissémination*, Seuil, 1972.

Gibson, Robert, *Modern French Poets on Poetry*, Cambridge University Press, 1961.

Kristeva, Julia, *La Révolution du langage poétique*, Seuil, 1974.

Mossop, D. J., *Pure Poetry. Studies in French Poetic Theory and Practice, 1746 to 1945*, Oxford, Clarendon Press, 1971.

Nordau, Max, *Entartung*, Berlin, Carl Dunder, 1892.

Zeitgenössische Franzosen, Berlin, Ernst Hoffman, 1901.

Paz, Octavio, *The Bow and the Lyre*, trans. Ruth L. C. Simms, McGraw-Hill, 1973.

Children of the Mire. Modern Poetry from Romanticism to the Avant-Garde, trans. Rachel Phillips, Harvard University Press, 1974.

Poulet, Georges, *La Distance Intérieure (Études sur le temps humain*, ii), Plon, 1952.

Les Métamorphoses du cercle, Plon, 1961.

Entre moi et moi. Essais critiques sur la conscience de soi, Corti, 1977.

Sartre, Jean-Paul, *Situations*, ix, Gallimard, 1972.

Scott, David H. T., *Sonnet Theory and Practice in Nineteenth-century France: Sonnets on the Sonnet*, Occasional Papers in Modern Languages, no. 12, Hull, University of Hull Publications, 1977.

Sewell, Elizabeth, *The Structure of Poetry*, Routledge and Kegan Paul, 1951.

Tolstoy, Leo, *What is Art?* and *Essays on Art*, trans. Aylmer Maude, Oxford University Press, 1930.

Weinberg, Bernard, *The Limits of Symbolism*, University of Chicago Press, 1966.

OTHER WORKS OF CRITICISM, LITERARY THEORY,
INTELLECTUAL HISTORY, ETC.

Banville, Théodore de, *Petit traité de poésie française* (1871), in *Œuvres*,
Lemerre, 1891.
Benveniste, Emile, *Problèmes de linguistique générale* [I], Gallimard, 1966.
Blum, Marcelle, *Le Thème symbolique dans le théâtre de Racine*, 2 vols, Nizet,
1962, 1965.
Bradley, A. C., *Oxford Lectures on Poetry*, Macmillan, 1909.
Burke, Kenneth, 'On Musicality in Verse', in *The Philosophy of Literary
Form,* Second Edition, Baton Rouge, Louisiana State University
Press, 1967.
Butler, Christopher, *Number Symbolism*, Routledge and Kegan Paul, 1970.
Chesters, Graham, *Some Functions of Sound-repetition in 'Les Fleurs du Mal'*,
Occasional Papers in Modern Languages, no. 11, Hull, University of
Hull Publications, 1975.
Cohen, Jean, *Structure du langage poétique*, Flammarion, 1966.
Coleman, Dorothy Gabe, *Maurice Scève: Poet of Love. Tradition and
Originality*, Cambridge University Press, 1975.
Collingwood, R. G., *The Principles of Art*, Oxford, Clarendon Press, 1938.
Culler, Jonathan, *Structuralist Poetics*, Routledge and Kegan Paul, 1975.
Davie, Donald, *Articulate Energy*, Routledge and Kegan Paul, 1955.
de Mourgues, Odette, *Metaphysical, Baroque and Précieux Poetry*, Oxford,
Clarendon Press, 1953.
Dodds, E. R., *The Greeks and the Irrational*, Berkeley and Los Angeles,
University of California Press, 1951.
Ehrenzweig, Anton, *The Hidden Order of Art*, Weidenfeld and Nicolson,
1967.
Einstein, Albert, *Relativity. The Special and the General Theory*, Methuen,
1954.
Eliot, T. S., *Selected Essays*, Faber and Faber, 1934.
Empson, William, *Seven Types of Ambiguity*, Second Edition, Chatto and
Windus, 1947.
Some Versions of Pastoral, Chatto and Windus, 1935.
Fairlie, Alison, '"Mène-t-on la foule dans les ateliers?"'—Some Remarks
on Baudelaire's Variants', in *Order and Adventure in Post-Romantic
French Poetry. Essays presented to C. A. Hackett*, ed. E. M. Beaumont,
J. M. Cocking and J. Cruickshank, Oxford, Blackwell, 1973, 17–37.
Fónagy, Ivan, 'The Functions of Vocal Style', in *Literary Style: a Symposium*,
ed. Seymour Chatman, Oxford University Press, 1971, 159–74.
Freud, Sigmund, *The Interpretation of Dreams*, The Standard Edition of the
Complete Psychological Works, ed. James Strachey, Vols IV and V,
Hogarth Press, 1953.
Jokes and their Relation to the Unconscious, Vol. VIII, 1960.
'Negation', Vol. XIX, 1961, 235–9.
Garnier, Pierre, *Spatialisme et poésie concrète*, Gallimard, 1968.
Genette, Gérard, *Figures II*, Seuil, 1969.
'Avatars du cratylisme', *Poétique*, no. 11, 1972, 367–94.

Mimologiques, Seuil, 1976.

Goldschmidt, Victor, *Essai sur le 'Cratyle'* (Bibliothèque de l'École des Hautes Études, no. 279), Champion, 1940.

Grammont, Maurice, *Le Vers français*, Third (revised) Edition, Champion, 1923.

Hackforth, R., *Plato's Phaedrus* (translation, introduction and commentary), Cambridge University Press, 1952.

Plato's Phaedo (translation, introduction and commentary), Cambridge University Press, 1955.

Hill, Archibald A. (review of works by Pierre Guiraud and Herbert Seidler), *Language*, Vol. 31, no. 2, April–June 1955, 249–52.

Hymes, Dell H., 'Phonological Aspects of Style', in Thomas A. Sebeok, ed., *Style in Language*, Cambridge, Mass., M.I.T. Press, 1960, 109–31.

Jakobson, Roman, 'Linguistics and Poetics', in Thomas A. Sebeok, ed., *Style in Language*, Cambridge, Mass., M.I.T. Press, 1960, 350–77.

'Poetry of Grammar and Grammar of Poetry', *Lingua*, Vol. 21, 1968, 597–609.

(with Lawrence G. Jones), *Shakespeare's Verbal Art in 'Th' expence of Spirit'*, The Hague, Mouton, 1970.

Questions de poétique, Seuil, 1973.

and Lévi-Strauss, Claude, '"Les Chats" de Charles Baudelaire', *L'Homme*, t.2, 1962, 5–21.

Jesperson, Otto, *The Philosophy of Grammar*, Allen and Unwin, 1924.

Jodogne, Pierre, 'Les "rhétoriqueurs" et l'humanisme: problème d'histoire littéraire', in *Humanism in France*, ed. A. H. T. Levi, Manchester, The University Press, 1970, 150–75.

Kirk, G. S. and Raven, J. E., *The Presocratic Philosophers*, Cambridge University Press, 1957.

Kuhn, Thomas S., *The Structure of Scientific Revolutions* (1962), Second Edition, University of Chicago Press, 1970.

Levin, Samuel R., *Linguistic Structures in Poetry*, The Hague, Mouton, 1962.

Lévi-Strauss, Claude and Jakobson, Roman, '"Les Chats" de Charles Baudelaire', *L'Homme*, t.2, 1962, 5–21.

Lewis, Roy, 'The Rhythmical Creation of Beauty', *Forum for Modern Language Studies*, Vol. VI, no. 2, April 1970, 103–26.

Lovejoy, Arthur O., *The Great Chain of Being*, New York, Harper and Row, 1960.

Mehlman, Jeffrey, *A Structural Study of Autobiography*, Cornell University Press, 1974.

Morier, Henri, *Dictionnaire de poétique et de rhétorique*, Presses Universitaires de France, 1961.

Murdoch, Iris, *The Fire and the Sun: Why Plato Banished the Artists*, Oxford, Clarendon Press, 1977.

Nowottny, Winifred, *The Language Poets Use*, The Athlone Press, 1962.

Panofsky, Erwin, *Idea. Ein Beitrag zur Begriffsgeschichte der älteren Kunsttheorie* (Studien der Bibliothek Warburg, 5), Leipzig–Berlin, 1924. (Translated as *Idea, a Concept in Art Theory*, by Joseph Peake, Columbia, University of South Carolina Press, 1968).

Pichois, Claude, ed., Baudelaire's *Œuvres complètes*, Vol. 1, 'Bibliothèque de la Pléiade', Gallimard, 1975.

Raven, J. E., *Plato's Thought in the Making*, Cambridge University Press, 1965.

Raven, J. E. and Kirk, G. S., *The Presocratic Philosophers*, Cambridge University Press, 1957.

Read, Herbert, *Collected Essays in Literary Criticism*, Second Edition, Faber and Faber, 1951.

Richard, Jean-Pierre, *Paysage de Chateaubriand*, Seuil, 1967.

Ricks, Christopher, *Milton's Grand Style*, Oxford, Clarendon Press, 1963.

Riffaterre, Michael, *Essais de stylistique structurale*, Flammarion, 1971.

Ross, W. D., *Plato's Theory of Ideas*, Oxford, Clarendon Press, 1951.

Ruwet, Nicolas, *Langage, musique, poésie*, Seuil, 1972.

Ryle, Gilbert, *Collected Papers*, Vol. 1, Hutchinson, 1971.

Saussure, Ferdinand de, *Cours de linguistique générale*, Troisième édition, Payot, 1972.

Sebeok, Thomas A., ed., *Style in Language*, Cambridge, Mass., M.I.T. Press, 1960.

Serres, Michel, *L'Interférence (Hermes II)*, Éditions de Minuit, 1972.

Smith, Barbara Herrnstein, *Poetic Closure*, University of Chicago Press, 1968.

Starobinski, Jean, *Les mots sous les mots: les anagrammes de Ferdinand de Saussure*, Gallimard, 1971.

Trilling, Lionel, *The Liberal Imagination* (1951), Harmondsworth, Peregrine Books, 1970.

Ullmann, Stephen, *Précis de sémantique française*, Berne, Éditions Francke, 1952.

Wellek, René and Warren, Austin, *Theory of Literature*, Third Edition, Harmondsworth, Peregrine Books, 1963.

Whitehead, Alfred North, *Science and the Modern World*, Cambridge University Press, 1926.

Wimsatt, W. K., 'One Relation of Rhyme to Reason', in *The Verbal Icon*, Lexington, University of Kentucky Press, 1954, 152–66.

Zumthor, Paul, *Langue, texte, énigme*, Seuil, 1975.

LITERARY AND PHILOSOPHICAL WORKS

Apollinaire, Guillaume, *Œuvres poétiques*, ed. Marcel Adéma and Michel Décaudin, 'Bibliothèque de la Pléiade', Gallimard, 1965.

Aragon, Louis, *Les Yeux d'Elsa*, London, Éditions Horizon-La France Libre, 1943.

Aristotle, *Poetics*, trans. Ingram Bywater, Oxford, Clarendon Press, 1920. (A new annotated translation is available in *Ancient Literary Criticism*, ed. D. A. Russell and M. Winterbottom, Oxford, Clarendon Press, 1972).

Metaphysics and *Topics* (Both available in translation in *The Works*, ed. J. A. Smith and W. D. Ross, Oxford, Clarendon Press, 1908–52.)

Bann, Stephen, *Concrete Poetry: an international anthology*, London Magazine
    Editions, 1967.
Baudelaire, Charles, *Œuvres complètes*, ed. Claude Pichois, Vol. 1,
    'Bibliothèque de la Pléiade', Gallimard, 1975.
Blake, William, *The Marriage of Heaven and Hell*, in *The Complete Writings*,
    ed. Geoffrey Keynes, Oxford University Press, 1966.
Cretin, Guillaume, *Œuvres poétiques*, ed. Kathleen Chesney, Firmin-Didot,
    1932.
Daniel, Samuel, *Poems* and *A Defence of Ryme*, ed. Arthur Colby Sprague,
    Phoenix Books, University of Chicago Press, 1965.
Du Bellay, Joachim, *La Deffence et illustration de la langue francoyse*, ed.
    Henri Chamard, *Société des textes français modernes*, Didier, 1948.
Ghil, René, *Les Dates et les Œuvres*, Éditions G. Crès et Cie, 1923.
Heraclitus, *The Cosmic Fragments*, ed. G. S. Kirk, Cambridge University
    Press, 1954.
Hopkins, Gerard Manley, 'On the Origin of Beauty: a Platonic Dialogue',
    in *The Note-Books and Papers of Gerard Manley Hopkins*, ed. Humphry
    House, Oxford University Press, 1937.
    The Poems, Fourth Edition, ed. W. H. Gardner and N. H. MacKenzie,
    Oxford University Press, 1967.
Horace, *Ars Poetica* (an annotated modern translation is available in
    Ancient Literary Criticism, ed. D. A. Russell and M. Winterbottom,
    Oxford, Clarendon Press, 1972).
Hugo, Victor, *La Légende des Siècles*, ed. Jacques Truchet, 'Bibliothèque
    de la Pléiade', Gallimard, 1950.
    Œuvres poétiques, ed. Pierre Albouy, Vol. 1, 'Bibliothèque de la Pléiade',
    Gallimard, 1964.
Johnson, Samuel, *The Rambler*, no. 94, in *Works*, Vol. IV, ed. W. J. Bate
    and Albrecht B. Strauss, Yale University Press, 1969.
Joyce, James, *Finnegans Wake*, Faber and Faber, 1964.
Keats, John, *The Poetical Works*, ed. H. W. Garrod, Oxford University
    Press, 1956.
Lamartine, Alphonse de, *Œuvres poétiques complètes*, ed. M.-F. Guyard,
    'Bibliothèque de la Pléiade', Gallimard, 1963.
Leibniz, G. W., *Die philosophischen Schriften*, ed. C. I. Gerhardt, Berlin,
    1875–90.
    The Monadology and Other Philosophical Writings, translated and
    introduced by Robert Latta, Oxford, Clarendon Press, 1898.
Leiris, Michel, *Glossaire j'y serre mes gloses* (1939), in *Mots sans mémoire*,
    Gallimard, 1969.
    Biffures (La Règle du jeu, Vol. 1), Gallimard, 1948.
Molinet, Jean, *Les Faictz et Dictz*, ed. Noël Dupire, Vol. 2, *Société des
    Anciens Textes Français*, 1937.
Pater, Walter, *Appreciations*, Macmillan, 1889.
Plato, *Cratylus, Euthyphro, Gorgias, Laws, Meno, Parmenides, Phaedo, Phaedrus,
    Protagoras, Republic, Symposium*. (The dialogues, translated by various
    hands, are now conveniently available in a single volume: *The
    Collected Dialogues*, ed. Edith Hamilton and Huntington Cairns,

Princeton, Princeton University Press, 1961.)

Plotinus, *The Enneads*, trans. Stephen MacKenna, Fourth Edition, Faber and Faber, 1969.

Pope, Alexander, *Peri Bathous* or *The Art of Sinking in Poetry*, reprinted in fascsimile, edited by Edna Leake Steeves, New York, King's Crown Press, Columbia University, 1952.

Proust, Marcel, *A la recherche du temps perdu*, ed. Pierre Clarac and André Ferré, 3 vols, 'Bibliothèque de la Pléiade', Gallimard, 1954.

Queneau, Raymond, *Cent mille milliards de poèmes*, Gallimard, 1961.

Rabelais, François, *Œuvres*, ed. Abel Lefranc, Vol. 2, Champion, 1913.

Reverdy, Pierre, *Main d'œuvre*, Mercure de France, 1949.

Roubaud, Jacques, ε, Gallimard, 1967.

Valéry, Paul, *Œuvres*, ed. Jean Hytier, 2 vols, 'Bibliothèque de la Pléiade', Gallimard, 1957, 1960.

Wordsworth, William, 'Ode: Intimations of Immortality from Recollections of Early Childhood', in *The Poetical Works*, ed. E. de Selincourt and Helen Darbishire, Vol. 4, Oxford, Clarendon Press, 1947.

INDEX

acrostics, 3
Albouy, Pierre, 169 n. 62
alexandrine, 7
allegory, 3, 10, 12–13, 32, 84, 124,
   129, 132, 179 n. 11
alliteration, 54, 56–62, 68–70, 75,
   83, 134–9, 140, 169, nn. 63,
   64
ambiguity, 8, 11, 35, 45, 63, 76, 87,
   88, 121–2, 139–40, 158 n. 8,
   166 n. 42, and *passim*
anagrams, 3, 65–6, 137–9, 145
analogy, 12, 68, 84
Apollinaire, Guillaume, 118, 120
apposition, 7, 34, 43, 56, 59
Aragon, Louis, 170 n. 69
Aristotle, 24, 79–80, 179 n. 16
   Poetics, 24
   Topics, 80
   Metaphysics, 179 n. 16
assonance, 54, 56–62, 68–70, 83,
   134–9, 140, 169 n. 64
Austin, J. L., 128
Austin, L. J., 32, 158 nn. 8, 9,
   163 nn. 19, 21, 22, 164 n. 27,
   169 n. 63, 175 n. 117, 180 n. 1
   (appendix)

Bach, J. S., 86
Bann, Stephen, 177 n. 4
Banville, Théodore de, 66, 67–8,
   170 n. 76, 171 n. 82
Barbier, Carl Paul, 163 n. 19, 181
   n. 1

Barthes, Roland, 82, 180 n. 27
Bate, W. J., 160 n. 4
Baudelaire, Charles, 4, 5, 29, 48,
   129–30, 159 n. 11, 168 n. 54,
   169 n. 64, 171 n. 78, 172 n. 87
Beaumont, E. M., 158 n. 8, 169 n.
   64
Béguin, Albert, 158 n. 9
Benda, Julien, 157 n. 1
Benveniste, Émile, 174 n. 111
Berma, La, 23
Bernard, Suzanne, 169 n. 67
Blake, William, 3, 127
Blanchot, Maurice, 143–4, 157 n. 2,
   175 n. 114, 178 n. 11, 180 n. 27
Blum, Marcelle, 172 n. 90
Bonnefoy, Yves, 158 n. 9, 178 n. 11
Borges, Jorge Luis, 91
Boulay, Daniel, 32, 162 n. 13
Bradley, A. C., 38
Burke, Kenneth, 57–8
Butler, Christopher, 179 n. 17

calligrammes, 118, 119–20
Campion, Thomas, 68
Carroll, Lewis, 118
'category mistakes', 51
causality, 85
Cazalis, Henri, 160 n. 9, 164 n. 32
Cebes, 79
Cellier, Léon, 163 n. 22
Chadwick, Charles, 163 n. 22, 178
   n. 11, 181 n. 1
Chamard, Henri, 171 n. 79

Champigny, Robert, 159 n. 10, 161 n. 9
chance, 65–6, 124–5, 127–8, 130, 140, 142, 143, 170 n. 75
Chateaubriand, François-René de, 176 n. 124
Chatman, Seymour, 175 n. 122
Chesney, Kathleen, 171 n. 80
Chesters, Graham, 171 n. 78, 172 n. 87
Chisholm, A. R., ix, 159 n. 10, 163 n. 22, 170 n. 77, 176 n. 2, 178 n. 11
Clarac, Pierre, 159 n. 1, 166 n. 44
Cocking, J. M., 158 n. 8, 169 n. 64
Cohen, Jean, 157 n. 2, 167 n. 48, 172 n. 93
Cohn, Robert Greer, 163 n. 22, 178 n. 11, 180 n. 24
Coleman, Dorothy Gabe, 179 n. 13
Coleridge, Samuel Taylor, 171 n. 79
Collingwood, R. G., 161 n. 10
communications, theory of, 43–4
compossibility, 47, 166 n. 43
concrete poetry, 119–20, 177 n. 4
contingency, 11, 26, 124, 127, 128, 132, 133, 142, 162 n. 15
contradiction, 12, 14–15, 17, 31, 46–7, 83, 84, 87, 89, 151
conundrums, 3
cratylism, 81–3, 138, 174 n. 113, 175 n. 114, 180 n. 22
Cretin, Guillaume, 67, 170 n. 71
Cruickshank, J., 158 n. 8, 169 n. 64
cryptograms, 58
cryptography, 3–4, 17

Daniel, Samuel, 68
Dante, 3
Da Ponte, Lorenzo, ii
Darbishire, Helen, 162 n. 17
Davie, Donald, 166 n. 40, 173 n. 99
Davies, Gardner, x, 158 n. 8, 163 nn. 19, 21, 177 n. 8, 179 nn. 11, 13, 20
death, 37, 89, 132, 152–4
decipherment, 3–4, 44, 78

Delfel, Guy, 161 n. 9, 175 n. 114, 178 n. 11
de Mourgues, Odette, 158 n. 1
de Selincourt, E., 162 n. 17
'depraved negative', 45, 165 n. 38
Derrida, Jacques, 178 n. 11
Descartes, René, 144, 180 n. 28
dialectic, 78, 79, 133, 143
Diotima, 28
Dodds, E. R., 161 n. 10, 162 n. 14
Donne, John, 3
Douchin, Jacques, 164 n. 22
Du Bellay, Joachim, 67
Duchesne-Guillemin, Jacques, 164 n. 22
Dumas, Olivier, 162 n. 13, 164 n. 22

Ehrenzweig, Anton, 16
Einstein, Albert, 144, 180 n. 28
Eliot, T. S., 40
Éluard, Paul, 122
Elwert, W. Th., 171 n. 85
Empson, William, 45, 87, 89, 166 n. 46
enactment, 6, 34, 45–6, 64, 74, 123, 165 n. 40, 167 n. 50
enjambement, 49, 72, 172 n. 85
epistemology, 4, 28–9, 85, 87–8, 119, 133, 135, 143, 151
etymology, 69, 77–8, 81–3, 174 n. 109

Fairlie, Alison, 159 n. 11, 169 n. 64
Faure, Gabriel, 162 n. 18
Ferré, André, 159 n. 1, 166 n. 44
Fónagy, Ivan, 175 n. 122
Forster, E. M., 89
Fraenkel, Ernest, 176 n. 2, 178 n. 11
Freud, Sigmund, 87, 149, 165 n. 38, 170 n. 68, 175 n. 120

Gadoffre, G. F. A., 158 n. 9
Gainsborough, Thomas, 151
Gans, Eric, 164 n. 22
Gardner, W. H., 167 n. 49
Garnier, Pierre, 120, 177 n. 4
Garrod, H. W., 180 n. 25
Gautier, Théophile, 11, 46

Genette, Gérard, 82, 161 n. 9, 167
   n. 48, 174 n. 113, 180 n. 22
Gerhardt, C. I., 166 n. 43
Ghil, René, 165 n. 37
Gibson, Robert, 165 n. 37
Gide, André, 176 n. 2
Gill, Austin, 163 n. 19
Goffin, Robert, 163 n. 22, 178 n. 11
Goldschmidt, Victor, 174 n. 110,
   175 n. 115
Góngora, Luis de, 3
Grammont, Maurice, 25, 49, 57–8
Greimas, A. J., 178 n. 11
Greville, Fulke, 3, 158 n. 1
Greyerz, Hans von, 164 n. 22, 171
   n. 77
Gualdo, Luigi, 181 n. 1
Guiraud, Pierre, 160 n. 6
Guyard, M.-F., 169 n. 62

Hackett, C. A., 158 n. 8, 169 n. 64
Hackforth, R., 162 n. 14, 174 n. 109
Hasidism, 1
Hayman, David, 173 n. 101
Hegel, Georg Wilhelm Friedrich,
   29, 163 n. 19
Heraclitus, 127
Herbert, George, 40, 118, 119
hermeticism, 38
Hermogenes, 81–2, 174 n. 113
hiatus, 5–8, 12, 17, 59–60, 84, 120–2,
   131, 134ff, 151
Hill, Archibald A., 160 n. 6
Holt, Eileen, 164 n. 27
homonymy, 54, 63–5, 78, 81, 83,
   131, 170 n. 72
homophony, 63–5, 68, 75
Hopkins, Gerard Manley, 55, 72,
   119, 167 n. 49, 168 n. 53
Horace, x, 165 n. 37
House, Humphry, 168 n. 53
Hugo, Victor, 3, 4, 5, 57, 118–19,
   169 n. 62
Hume, David, 142
Huysmans, J.-K., 163 n. 21
Hymes, Dell H., 57–8
hyperbole, 33, 36–7, 40, 166 n. 46
Hytier, Jean, 159 n. 2, 165 n. 40,

169 nn. 62, 66, 174 n. 107,
   176 n. 1

ideal, the, 13–15, 26–30, 33–7, 40–1,
   45–6, 64–5, 72, 74, 76–8, 78–81,
   85, 158 n. 9
idealism, 9, 26–30, 76–8, 81
Ideas, the, 14, 26–30, 34–7, 64–5,
   74, 79–81, 130, 161 nn. 9, 11,
   174 n. 106
ideograms, 118, 176 n. 2
illocutionary forces, 128
imagery, 4, 10–13, 33–7, 46–7,
   125–6, 134, 140–2, 153, 159
   n. 10, 160 n. 6, 161 n. 11, 172
   n. 87
information, 15–16, 43–4, 49, 54,
   56, 70, 152
iridaceae, 85, 175 n. 117
Iris pseudacorus, 175 n. 117
irony, 30, 40, 41, 120, 127, 133, 161
   n. 10

Jakobson, Roman, 54–6, 168 n. 54,
   170 n. 75
Jean-Aubry, G., viii, 158 n. 3
Jespersen, Otto, 173 n. 98
Jodogne, Pierre, 171 n. 80
Johnson, Samuel, 24, 160 n. 4
Jones, Lawrence G., 168 n. 54
Joyce, James, 78, 151, 173 n. 101

Keats, John, 141
Keynes, Geoffrey, 179 n. 15
Kirk, G. S., 179 n. 16
Kravis, Judy, 170 n. 67, 171 n. 82
Kristeva, Julia, 88–9, 163 n. 22,
   175 n. 122, 176 n. 123, 178 n. 11
Kuhn, Thomas S., 158 n. 2

Lamartine, Alphonse de, 169 n. 62
Latta, Robert, 166 n. 43
Lawrenson, T. E., 158 n. 9
Lefébure, Eugène, 30–1
Lefranc, Abel, 171 n. 81
Leibniz, Gottfried Wilhelm, 47, 166
   n. 43

Leiris, Michel, 138–9, 179 n. 21,
  180 n. 22
Levi, A. H. T., 171 n. 80
Levin, Samuel R., 168 nn. 54, 56
Lévi-Strauss, Claude, 168 n. 54
Lewis, Roy, 168 n. 61, 171 n. 83
logic, 15, 51, 71, 81, 121, 128, 131,
  144, 154, 159 nn. 10, 11
Lovejoy, Arthur O., 26, 85–6
Lucretius, 3

MacKenna, Stephen, 161 n. 11
MacKenzie, N. H., 167 n. 49
Mallarmé, Stéphane (individual
  works by),
  'A la nue accablante tu', 124–7,
    178 n. 11
  'Au seul souci de voyager', 72,
    124, 178 n. 11
  'Billet à Whistler', 72
  'Crise de vers', 82–3, 169 n. 67
  'Dans le jardin', 164 n. 27
  'Hérésies artistiques : l'art pour
    tous', 38–9
  'Hérodiade', 165 n. 33
  'Hommage' (to Puvis de
    Chavannes), 170 n. 72
  'Hommage' (to Wagner), 7–8
  Igitur, 124–6
  La Musique et les lettres, 130
  L'Après-midi d'un faune, 5–6
  'Le Pitre châtié', 158 n. 8
  'Le vierge, le vivace et le bel
    aujourd'hui', 9–13, 15, 31,
    135, 153–4, 159 n. 10, 160 n. 6,
    172 n. 86
  'Prose pour Cazalis', 164 n. 32
  'Prose pour des Esseintes', viii,
    ix, xi, 5, 6, 13–15, 19–89, 123,
    133, 134, 150, 153–4, 155–6,
    159 nn. 10, 11, 160 n. 9, 162
    n. 13, 163 nn. 21, 22, 165 n. 33,
    166 n. 46, 169 n. 64, 170 n. 77,
    173 n. 97, 175 nn. 117, 122,
    180 n. 1 (appendix)
  'Prose pour des Esseintes' (earlier
    version), 155–6, 159 n. 11, 166
    n. 46, 169 n. 64, 180–1 n. 1

'Quand l'ombre menaça de la
  fatale loi', 6
'Réponse à Jules Huret', 169
  n. 67
'Salut' ('Rien, cette écume,
  vierge vers'), 124, 178 n. 11
'Ses purs ongles très haut
  dédiant leur onyx', 7
'Solennité', 171 n. 82
'Toast funèbre', 46, 170 n. 72
'Toute l'âme résumée', 72
*Un Coup de dés jamais n'abolira le
  hasard*, viii, ix, xi, 5, 91–145,
  150, 153–4, 173 n. 101, 176
  nn. 1, 2, 177 nn. 3, 7, 8, 178
  n. 11, 180 nn. 24, 26, 27
vers de circonstance, 150, 171 n. 85
Marino, Giambattista, 3
Marvell, Andrew, 3, 40, 48, 165
  n. 35, 166 n. 46
Maude, Aylmer, 179 n. 14
Mauron, Charles, 178 n. 11
Mehlman, Jeffrey, 180 n. 22
memory, 28–9, 33, 162 n. 15
Merrill, Stuart, 169 n. 63
metaphor, 12, 131, 132, 138, 166
  n. 42
metaphysical poets, the, 40–1
metaphysics, x–xi, 9, 13, 25–30,
  34–7, 39, 65, 76, 78–81, 84,
  119, 126–30, 153, 160 n. 9,
  161 n. 11
metonymy, 7, 64
metre, metrics, 7, 14, 23, 25, 49–53,
  56, 58, 59, 60, 62, 68, 121,
  126, 153, 167 nn. 48, 49, 171
  n. 85
Milton, John, 3, 122, 166 n. 42,
  178 n. 9
mimesis, 24, 118–20, 151, 165 n. 40,
  174 n. 113, 176 n. 2
modernism, 5, 16, 26, 151
Molinet, Jean, 63–4, 67, 170 n. 71
Mondor, Henri, viii, 40, 158 n. 3,
  161 n. 9, 163 nn. 20, 22, 169
  n. 63, 176 n. 2, 180 n. 1
  (appendix)
Morier, Henri, 171 n. 82

Mossop, D. J. 163–4 n. 22, 165
n. 33, 178 n. 11
Mozart, Wolfgang Amadeus, ii,
154
Murdoch, Iris, 161 n. 10
music, musicality, 46, 50, 57, 58,
60–1, 67, 69, 76, 84, 120, 149,
167 n. 49, 168 nn. 54, 61, 169
n. 67

negativity, 152–3
neo-Platonism, 27, 29, 161 n. 11
Nerval, Gérard de, 4
Newton, Isaac, 9
Nordau, Max, 157 n. 1
Noulet, Émilie, ix, 163 n. 22, 170
n. 77, 178 n. 11, 179 n. 13
Nowottny, Winifred, 167 n. 50,
172 n. 96
number, 3, 126, 129–32, 140, 179
n. 17

obscurity, ix–x, 13, 38–9, 41, 157
n. 2, 158 n. 1, 165 n. 33
onomatopœia, 25, 29
'otherworldiness', 26, 30, 79, 85,
160 n. 7
overdetermination, 139–42, 152

Panofsky, Erwin, 161 n. 11
paradigm-shifts, 4, 158 n. 2
paradox, 7, 10, 17, 33, 45
Parent, Monique, 171 n. 85
Parmenides, 80, 173 n. 104
Pater, Walter, 166 n. 45
Paz, Octavio, 180 n. 26
Peake, Joseph, 162 n. 11
periphrasis, 41–2, 47–8
Phillips, Rachel, 180 n. 26
Pichois, Claude, 168 n. 54, 179 n. 18
Plato, 26–30, 40, 78–83, 160 n. 7,
161 nn. 9, 10, 11, 162 nn. 13,
14, 164 n. 22, 168 n. 53, 173
nn. 103, 104, 174 nn. 106, 109,
110, 113, 175 nn. 114, 115
Cratylus, 81–3, 174 nn. 109, 110,
113, 175 nn. 114, 115
Euthyphro, 28

Gorgias, 79
Laws, 174 n. 108
Meno, 28, 161 n. 10
Parmenides, 79–81, 173 n. 104
Phaedo, 28, 79, 160 n. 7, 162 nn.
13, 14, 174 n. 109
Phaedrus, 28, 79, 161 n. 10, 162
n. 13, 174 n. 109
Protagoras, 79
Republic, 27, 161 n. 10
Symposium, 28
pleasure, 3, 4, 16–17, 62, 71, 145,
149, 170 n. 68, 171 n. 82
Plotinus, 27, 161 n. 11
Poe, Edgar Allan, 29
polarity, 12, 15, 34, 64, 72–3, 76–7,
79, 84, 175 n. 120
polysemy, 63, 121
Pope, Alexander, 42, 78
Poulet, Georges, 32, 162 n. 15
Pound, Ezra, 118
pre-existence, 28–9
Proust, Marcel, 23–4, 47, 83, 162
n. 15, 174 n. 112
Puvis de Chavannes, Pierre, 170
n. 72
Pythagoreans, the, 129, 179 n. 16

Queneau, Raymond, 118

Rabelais, François, 67
Racine, Jean, 59, 172 n. 90
Raitt, Alan, 163 n. 19
Raven, J. E., 162 n. 16, 173 nn. 103,
104, 179 n. 16
Read, Herbert, viii
Recollection (Plato's doctrine of),
27–9
Rembrandt, 154
Requiem mass, 50
Reverdy, Pierre, 122, 178 n. 10
rhétoriqueurs, les grands, 66–7,
171 nn. 78, 80
rhyme, 23, 25, 49, 54, 60–1, 62, 64,
66–78, 83, 84, 85, 123, 131,
170 nn. 68, 72, 76, 77, 171 nn.
78, 79, 82, 85, 172 nn. 86, 87,
88, 90, 93, 94, 96, 173 nn. 97, 99

rhythm, 7, 24, 53, 75, 84, 88, 144, 153, 167 n. 49, 168 n. 61, 171 nn. 83, 85, 172 n. 87, 176 n. 2
Richard, Jean-Pierre, ix, 32, 89, 161 n. 9, 163 nn. 19, 20, 166 n. 46
Ricks, Christopher, 166 n. 42, 178 n. 9
Riley, Bridget, 151
Ross, W. D., 174 n. 106
Roubaud, Jacques, 118
Roulet, Claude, 176 n. 2, 178 n. 11
Ryle, Gilbert, 173 n. 104

Sartre, Jean-Paul, 178 n. 11
Saussure, Ferdinand de, 62, 65–6, 82, 170 nn. 74, 75, 174 n. 111
Scève, Maurice, 3, 158 n. 1, 179 n. 13
Scherer, Jacques, 165 n. 37, 178 n. 11
Schoenberg, Arnold, 151
science, 4, 17, 24, 28, 85, 129, 158 n. 2, 160 n. 6
Scott, David H. T., 159 n. 10, 165 39, 179 n. 13
Sebeok, Thomas A., 168 nn. 51, 59
Seidler, Herbert, 160 n. 6
Serres, Michel, 87–8
Sewell, Elizabeth, 159 n. 10, 179 n. 11
Shakespeare, 48, 147, 168 n. 54
Shawcross, J., 171 n. 79
Simmias, 79
Simms, Ruth L. C., 180 n. 26
Smith, Barbara Herrnstein, 166 n. 41, 168 n. 55
Socrates, 27, 28, 79, 81–2, 162 n. 13, 174 n. 113
sound-patterning, 7, 10, 24–5, 40, 53–78, 81, 84, 88, 134–9, 140, 142, 153, 159 n. 10, 160 n. 4, 160 n. 6, 169 nn. 63, 64, 67, 171 nn. 78, 83
'sound symbolism', 25, 58
space, 10, 76, 116, 117–24, 126, 128, 135, 144–5, 153, 160 n. 6, 176 n. 2, 177 nn. 3, 7, 8, 180 n. 27

Sprague, Arthur Colby, 171 n. 84
Starobinski, Jean, 65–6, 170 nn. 74, 75
Steeves, Edna Leake, 165 n. 36
Strachey, James, 165 n. 38, 170 n. 68, 175 n. 120
Strauss, Albrecht B., 160 n. 4
structure, 12, 19, 29, 39, 48, 79, 84, 86, 87, 123, 126, 127, 128, 129, 131–2, 133, 140, 142, 143, 157 n. 2, 166 n. 41, 167 n. 50, 169 n. 67, 170 n. 75, 173 n. 99, 176 n. 123, 179 n. 11
Sutcliffe, F. E., 158 n. 9
syllogism, 128
symbolism, 3, 161 n. 11, 176 n. 122, 179 n. 17
Symbolism ('*Le Symbolisme*'), 26, 167 n. 48, 179 n. 11
syntax, 5–8, 10–12, 14, 24, 34, 36, 43–53, 56, 58, 59, 62, 74, 83, 84, 88, 120–4, 126, 127, 128, 134, 135, 137, 138, 139–40, 141–2, 144, 153, 165 nn. 37, 40, 166 nn. 41, 42, 45, 167 n. 48, 171 n. 85, 173 nn. 97, 99, 177 n. 8, 178 n. 9, 179 n. 11

taxonomy, 39, 85
Thibaudet, Albert, 160 n. 6, 171 n. 78, 172 n. 85
'this-worldliness', 26, 86
Tolstoy, Leo, 125, 157 n. 1
transcendence, 9, 28–9, 33, 36, 74, 78, 83, 127, 138, 162 n. 13, 166 n. 46
Trilling, Lionel, 149
Truchet, Jacques, 168 n. 58
typography, 116–24, 176 n. 2, 177 nn. 3, 7, 8

Ullmann, Stephen, 63, 170 n. 71
unconscious, the, 16, 88–9, 170 n. 68, 175 n. 122, 176 nn. 123, 2

variants, 159 n. 11, 164 n. 22, 166 n. 46, 169 n. 64
Valéry, Paul, 23–4, 48, 59, 60, 81,

83, 117–18, 165 n. 40, 169
n. 62, 171 n. 78, 176 n. 2
Verdin, Simonne, 163 n. 22, 178
n. 11
Verhoeff, J. P., 32, 164 n. 26
Vinaver, Eugène, 158 n. 9
Voltaire, 142

Wagner, Richard, 7
Walzer, Pierre-Olivier, 164 n. 22,
170 n. 77
Warren, Austin, 172 n. 88
Weinberg, Bernard, 179 n. 11

Wellek, René, 172 n. 88
Whistler, James McNeill, 172 n. 91
Whitehead, A. N., 85
Wimsatt, W. K., 71, 172 n. 89
Woolf, Virginia, 19
word-play, 63–5, 66–8, 77–8, 81, 83,
137–9, 170 n. 68, 171 nn. 81, 82,
83, 173 n. 101, 174 n. 109
Wordsworth, William, 9, 29, 53

Yeats, W. B., 149

Zumthor, Paul, 171 n. 81